UNDERSTANDING

DIRECT ACCESS

TRADING

UNDERSTANDING DIRECT ACCESS TRADING

Making the Move from Your Online Broker
to Direct Access Trading

Rafael Romeu

McGraw-Hill
New York   Chicago   San Francisco
Lisbon   London   Madrid   Mexico City   Milan
New Delhi   San Juan   Seoul   Singapore
Sydney   Toronto

Library of Congress Cataloging-in-Publication Data

Romeu, Rafael
   Understanding direct access trading :   making the move from your online broker to direct assess trading / by Rafael Romeu.
      p.   cm.
   ISBN 0-07-136250-9
   1. Electronic trading of securities   2. Investments—Computer network resources.
   3. Investments—Information services.   I. Title.

HG4515.95 .R663 2000
332.63'2'02854678—dc21

00-053701

McGraw-Hill

A Division of The McGraw-Hill Companies

1 2 3 4 5 6 7 8 9 0   AGM/AGM   0 7 6 5 4 3 2 1

ISBN 0-07-136250-9

The sponsoring editor for this book was Stephen Isaacs, the editing supervisor was Ruth W. Mannino, and the production supervisor was Charles Annis.

Printed and bound by Quebecor/Martinsburg.

This publication is designed to provide accurate and authoritative information in regard to the subject matter covered. It is sold with the understanding that neither the author nor the publisher is engaged in rendering legal, accounting, or other professional service. If legal advice or other expert assistance is required, the services of a competent professional person should be sought.
—*From a Declaration of Principles jointly adopted by a Committee of the American Bar Association and a Committee of Publishers*

The viewpoints and content expressed by the author are his own and not those of Trade scape.com, Inc. or any of its affiliated entities, employees, officers, directors, or authorized representatives (the "Company"). The company does not endorse any of the content contained herein and has not verified the accuracy of any of the content. The information is not to be construed as investment advice and any reliance on the content as contained herein is at the reader's sole risk and liability.

Tradescape1.0™ and TradescapePro™ are trademarks of Tradescape.com, Inc.; Nex-Trade™, of NexTrade Holdings, Inc.; and Ameritrade™, of Ameritrade, Inc. Island® is a registered trademark of The Island ECN, Inc. and E*TRADE® of E*TRADE, Inc. All other trademarked products mentioned are used in an editorial fashion only, and to the benefit of the trademark owner, with no intention of infringement of the trademark. Where such designations appear in this book, they have been printed with initial caps.

*In recognition of the thirtieth anniversary of
Jorge Luis and Zoila Romeu*

Feliz Trigésimo Aniversario

CONTENTS

PREFACE

Understanding Direct Access Trading is part of a six-book series on direct access trading from McGraw-Hill. The series of books represents the first detailed look at every element of direct access trading for individuals interested in harnessing the amazing changes occurring in the world's financial markets. All the books contain a clear and basic approach on how to take advantage of direct access to the markets for your specific level of investing/trading. Direct access trading is for everyone, and in this series of books, we show you how to take advantage of it if you only place a couple of trades a year, if you are just starting to get more active in the markets, or even if you want to be a day trader. Take advantage of these revolutionary changes today, and start accessing the markets directly with direct access trading. Good luck!

ACKNOWLEDGMENTS

I would like to thank Jorge Luis B. Romeu, Ricardo Romeu, and my parents for their suggestions and invaluable encouragement. I am grateful to Carmen Reinhart and Roger Betancourt for supporting me in this project. I would like to thank Jonathan Aspatore for the opportunity to write this book and José Pineda and Umar Serajuddin for their comments and suggestions. I would like to recognize William D. Carlisle, Adam De-Sanctis, Francisco Vázquez, Taryn Roeder, Edgar A. Chávez, Fernando Verdasco, and Patrick T. Collins for their encouragement. My thanks to my family and to all the individuals who have contributed to or supported me in the writing of this book.

1

WHAT THIS BOOK WILL DO FOR YOU

There seems to be a persistent doubt among a large segment of the population regarding whether they are missing out on investment opportunities. Many of us, for example, have savings sitting in an account or perhaps a CD. We may suspect that while we are getting feeble returns from our savings accounts, we are letting pass a wealth of opportunities in the stock markets. We sit mesmerized on the sidelines while we hear of everyday people making a killing from investing in the stock markets. Those who are investing have an advantage in saving for retirement or for their children's education, a vacation home, or many other transactions requiring significant amounts of money. And more likely than not, what is stopping us from trying to participate in this type of investment is the inability to find clear explanations of how and where to get involved in the financial markets. Who among us doesn't have a friend, neighbor, or acquaintance who appears to un-

derstand the markets to their core and is reaping profits from them? Meanwhile, we continue on the sidelines, feeling powerless to act because we may feel that we do not have adequate training and experience to safely invest in the mammoth stock markets.

Some of us know of or have online investment accounts sitting idle while the markets fluctuate back and forth. We know some things about buying stocks but feel like the randomness of the markets is enough to make one back off and invest very conservatively. We may look at investing in a company like putting money into a black box and, hopefully, getting more money back. Moreover, when we hear Wall Street professionals and insiders talk, it seems that they understand what is going on in the mysterious Wall Street black box and how money is made. It would seem that these professionals know where to invest their money, and they have the ability to predict which stocks will be good investments, whereas we invest based on a combination of hope, guessing, luck, and the rumor mill. With disadvantages like these, it only makes sense to keep out of the markets.

We even may have heard of day traders who make a living from trading back and forth all day in the markets. It would seem, or at least some of the reports would have us believe, that someone who does this for a living is an extreme risk taker. The character of day trading is often portrayed to be one of instability, as if at any moment a day trader could be wiped out and destitute. Day trading is sometimes blamed for instability and fluctuations in the market. Like the other reasons, this kind of day trading would seem to be incompatible with the type of investment that most of us picture ourselves engaging in.

There is, however, an innovation. There is a technology that has made the stock markets readily accessible to small investors at reasonable prices. The purpose of this book is to serve as a source for individuals to bridge the gaps in their knowledge of the stock markets and of how to gain access to them through this breakthrough technology. The book addresses the issue of which opportunities are available to small investors looking to enter the stock markets and how a new technology called *electronic direct access trading* sharply increases the range of opportunities. In other words, the idea is to take away the mystique of the stock markets, to try to explain how and where profits are made, to show how professionals working on Wall Street derive their profits, and to help clarify some of the vagueness of how to invest in stocks.

In this effort, the approach to explaining the new opportunities for small investors in the stock markets is two-pronged. The first part of every explanation is to show how trading actually occurs, what is being traded, what mediums or technology is used to trade, and who controls the mediums. Understanding the trading requires an understanding of the persons, institutions, and events that collectively make up the stock markets. In doing so, the book uses plain language and simple ideas to explain the unusual jargon of Wall Street. The purpose of this is not to back away from financial terms but rather to bring them down to earth, because many times the words are much more complicated than the ideas they represent.

The second part of explaining these new opportunities for investors is to show why trading occurs the way it does. That is, we can describe what alternatives are available to different individuals who trade on the stock markets. The more relevant question becomes, Why do individuals choose certain alternatives sometimes, or why do they engage in certain types of trading? To answer this, we look at the costs and benefits resulting from the different choices that traders can make. Everyone invests with the same overarching incentive, which is to make money. By looking at the costs and benefits, we can see where individuals make the most amount of money and can understand the incentives they have for making the investment choices they make. Just following the money reveals a tremendous amount about why stock prices behave the way they do and where the opportunities lie for small investors with direct access to the markets.

The general information contained in this book is intended to first lay down the basics of the stock markets so as to paint a fairly complete picture of the opportunities for a small investor. The book begins by assuming that the reader knows very little about investing and then tells the story of where and how investment opportunities can be found in the stock markets today. The intended readers are both individuals trying to improve the return on their investments from traditional stockbrokers or online brokerages and individuals who have money sitting in the bank and no involvement in the stock markets but who want to know more about how to invest efficiently.

There are eight chapters in this book, this being the first one. Chapter 2 looks at an overview of the financial system in general, which includes the stock market as well as other financial markets. This chapter is intended to give a brief bird's eye view of what the financial system is and some of the most important relationships present in it. This chapter is intended as background and may be skipped without loss of continuity. Chapter 3 looks at the context of investing and how the system of buying stock in a company works. The major mediums for buying stocks and participating in the markets are described in this chapter, e.g., stockbrokers. Chapter 4 presents the structure of stock markets in general and outlines the differences and similarities between the New York Stock Exchange and the Nasdaq. Together these three chapters present the environment available for individuals to invest their savings.

Chapter 5 addresses head-on what electronic direct access trading is and what the potential benefits are to using this medium of trading. The chapter describes the sources of the benefits to using electronic direct access and what it is about this form of investing that generates better returns to investing. Chapter 6 covers the effect of information on the return to trading and investing. That is, it looks at how price movements and financial news such as earnings expectations influence the markets or the herd of traders and investors putting money in the markets. Chapter 7 looks at how the major players in the markets function in general. That is, we partition the group of investors buying and selling stocks into general groups and describe how the members of each group generally trade based on how each group makes money on Wall Street. These two chapters together describe how the influences that are brought to bear on the markets move the herd of traders around and affect profits for everyone.

Chapter 8 describes the different types of Internet-based investment vehicles that are available to small investors. This chapter shows the actual trading screens and technology that investors use and that we call electronic direct access trading. Chapter 9 wraps up the book with a series of frequently asked questions about all aspects of electronic direct access trading, as well as about the contents of the book. Colleagues who are also at the forefront of the electronic direct access trading technology provided the answers to the questions. The idea of this chapter is that by including the input of others involved in the field, the total picture of the investment opportunities presented in this book will be richer and more broadly based.

AN OVERVIEW OF THE FINANCIAL SYSTEM

The purpose of this chapter is to give a very general outline of the financial system. The stock market is only one medium of investing money, and it does not exist in a vacuum. It functions in parallel competition with other markets that actively compete for money. That is, the savings that people have available for investment will be diverted to some part of the financial system. The stock market is just one part of the financial system that the savings of everyday people could end up in, but there are other markets for these savings. This chapter will look at the big picture of investing and the different markets that exist and which try to lure investment dollars to them. There are many general questions relevant to the big picture of the financial system, e.g., Why are there many alternatives to the stock market, and what do these alternatives represent? How do they make their money? What are the relative advantages and disadvantages to using these mediums of in-

vesting instead of the stock markets? Having a general overview of the financial system will help clarify the answers to some of these questions. It is helpful to know these answers; they are important to every investor. Having said this, the reality is that there are always many more questions and answers that are worth knowing. This chapter relates issues that may be skipped by the reader who is pressed for time, and the book will continue without discontinuity. That is, for a direct and exclusive look at direct access trading, the reader may skip over this chapter and read it at a later time.

Very generally, when I say the *financial system,* I am referring to the vast network of institutions and individuals who work in buying and selling money. That is, the financial system is just all the banks and similar types of businesses, as well as private investors, and local, state, and federal government agencies that are involved in the process of providing money for those businesses and individuals who need it. Thus, for example, a loan officer approving a mortgage loan to someone looking to buy a house is part of the financial system, as is a local government issuing a bond to build a school or a bank in New York City selling certificates of deposit to its customers.

These businesses and individuals all engage in the buying and selling of money, as stated previously. Obviously, buying money is not like buying a car, or a house, or a tomato because the price of all these things is specified in money. Thus, if we use money to buy things like cars, houses, or tomatoes, what do we use to buy money itself? It would not make much sense to buy a dollar using four quarters. Banks like Citibank or Chase Manhattan cannot thrive on making change for people alone. The answer is that banks buy and sell money and pay interest on the money they buy or earn interest when they sell money. In effect, the *interest rate* is the price of money. We can think of the price of money as being the rate at which money is gained or lost due to engaging in the transaction of buying and selling money. Thus, for example, if we buy a car and it costs $1000, then the price of the car is the amount of money we give up in acquiring it. If we buy a $10,000 loan from a bank and the bank charges us 7 percent interest on the loan, then the price of money becomes the 7 percent interest on the $10,000. The 7 percent interest that we pay on the loan is the amount of money we give up in acquiring the loan. As a result, the interest paid on the $10,000 loan is the amount of money we give up in order to acquire the $10,000 loan. It is the same concept as giving up $1000 for the ownership of a car, except that instead of owning a car, we own a $10,000 loan. This is why the price of money is the interest rate.

The interest rate is a very important price in the economy. By defining the price of money, it is the price of having liquidity in the economy. That is, at any given point in time, there is only a certain amount of actual cash and savings available for businesses and individuals to borrow. The actual amount available can depend on how much people are in need of money, how much they are willing to save, how much of their earnings they can forgo, and how much money they expect they will make in the future. When I say that people pay for money because they need liquidity, I am referring to the fact that people may have their wealth tied up in illiquid assets but need to pay off a bill right away, so they borrow to tap into their wealth and gain liquidity. For example, suppose there was a farmer with 500,000 acres planted, but the harvest was 2 months away. If the farmer needed to pay a debt immediately, he or she would need to tap into the value of the future harvest. That is, the farmer is wealthy enough to pay off the debt because the harvest will generate plenty of income, but the farmer's wealth is tied up in the harvest, and cannot be accessed until harvest time comes. As a result, the farmer may borrow to gain liquidity and pay off the debt. As the need for more money increases, the farmer will be willing to pay a higher interest rate to borrow and to pay off the debt. As there is more money available, because many people are saving money in their savings accounts and banks have a lot of cash to loan out, the interest rate will be less, and the farmer will have a lower cost of borrowing.

The need for money and the supply of money available are the core problems with which the entire financial system deals. The interest rate reflects the demand and supply of money. It is for this reason that interest rates are so important and why they affect many financial markets, including the stock market. In understanding the financial system, it is crucial to have a basic understanding of interest rates. The easiest way to conceptualize the movements of the interest rates and what effects they have on the rest of the financial system in general, and the prospects of a small investor in particular, is by looking at the bond market.

There is a kind of financial instrument that almost everyone has heard of called a *bond*. We can think of a bond as simply a piece of paper that you buy, and by holding it, you are entitled to receive certain payments in the future. That is, a bond is essentially a piece of paper that you cannot buy things with. For example, you cannot walk into the corner store and pay for a carton of milk with a bond. As a result, by buying a bond, we give up the ability to purchase other things, and the purchasing power of the money we use to pay for the bond goes to the person selling the bond to us. We transfer our purchasing power to the bond issuer in exchange for the bond. For example, many people may buy U.S. Savings Bonds. In doing so, they are giving up cash that could be used to buy items at the store and instead are handing the cash over to the government. The government then gives these bond buyers the piece of paper that we call a U.S. Savings Bond. The individual holding this piece of paper is entitled to certain payments in the future. It is for this reason that bond markets are an interesting phenomenon. The bond is nothing more than a fancy IOU (IOU is short for "I owe you") from the government to the buyer of the bond. And it is not just the government that sells bonds; many corporations also write up their own bonds, i.e., their own IOUs, and sell them to get a hold of people's money. Basically, any organization with the ability to issue an IOU to the public and credibly sell it can issue a bond. In this way, any organization that has the credibility to issue bonds and can get people to buy them can borrow from the public through the bond market, be they a local government, a corporation, or some other organization. As long as they can find an individual who will give up hard-earned cash in exchange for the kind of IOU that we call a bond, they can sell this individual a bond and in doing so raise funds immediately. Again, notice that a person who buys a bond is not buying other things, such as cars or other items, in particular other financial products, such as stocks. This is why the money that is available for the bond market depends on how much people are willing to forgo spending money on consumption items or other financial products with which bonds compete. As the issuer of a bond attempts to raise funds by selling bonds, the money that the issuer can tap into depends on how much money people are willing to lend, instead of spending it on themselves at the mall, for example.

It comes as no surprise that we call the markets where bonds are bought and sold the *bond markets*. Bond markets are similar to stock markets in the sense that they are a financial market where certain instruments are bought and sold and in the process buyers and sellers agree on a price. The interesting and important fact about bond markets is that *they are where the interest rates are determined*. That is, the price at which individuals are buying and selling bonds has a direct effect on how interest rates are moving. In fact, interest rates are determined directly by the prices for which bonds are selling in bond markets. This may not be obvious at first glance, but we can see that this is the case by looking at how the market for bonds works.

First, we can look at three kinds of bonds; they are *discount bonds*, *fixed-rate bonds*, and *coupon bonds*. A bond is like a loan, so it is helpful to think of the different characteristics that these three kinds of bonds have as different characteristics that one may have pertaining to a loan from a bank. All bonds have a *face value*, i.e., a number written on the bond that says how much the bond is worth on a certain date in the future, called the *date of maturity*. If this were a loan from a bank, the face value would be something like the principal owed to the bank on the loan. Thus, if you have a bond with a face value of $1000, at maturity, that bond is worth $1000. Similarly, if you had a loan with a face value of $1000, you would owe the bank $1000 at some point. Some bonds also include as part of their payoff a *coupon*, which is a payment made to the holder of the bond before maturity. The coupon payment is made periodically, e.g., every year. In a loan situation, the coupon would be like the interest payments made to the bank. Thus, for example, a bond with a $1000 face value that matures in 10 years may make a yearly coupon payment of $100. In this case, the bond has a 10 percent coupon rate. This means that the bond pays the holder $100 every year, as well as $1000 on the last year. Some bonds do not have coupons, which means that they do not pay anything in the time between when they are issued and when they mature; they only pay on the date of maturity. If this were a loan, we could think of it as borrowing some amount from the bank and then making one big payment to the bank at some point in the future to pay the entire loan back plus interest.

Bonds, as I said before, are just pieces of paper that people give up cash for today and get cash from tomorrow. There are many different kinds of bonds, so they are usually described in terms of their characteristics, such as face value, how long one has to wait before they mature, their coupon rate, and the issuer. The three kinds of bonds mentioned earlier are just three ways in which the issuer of a bond can make payments on the face value and the coupon rate. A discount bond, for example, has no coupon. This is why it is sometimes also called a *zero-coupon bond*. As such, a discount bond with a face value of $1000 pays $1000 on the date it matures. It is called a *discount bond* because the price is less than the face value, or discounted. Thus, for example, a

$1000 face-value discount bond with 10 years to maturity may sell for $500. This just means that an investor can pay $500 now for a piece of paper that entitles the holder to receive $1000 ten years from now. If this were a loan, it would be like borrowing $500 and paying back $1000 in 5 years, for example. Notice that the return to this investment is $500, i.e., 100 percent, because the initial investment was $500, and the return was $500. We call the return rate that equates the price of the bond to the present value of the money that the bond will pay in the future the *yield*. The idea behind the yield for a bond is as follows: Suppose we ask the following question: Given that the discount bond described earlier costs $500 and pays back $1000, what would the interest rate on a bank account have to be for one to be indifferent between buying the bond and putting the money in the bank? The answer is that the bank would have to pay 100 percent interest on the $500 to make the person indifferent between buying the bond and depositing the money. For this reason, the yield for this discount bond is 100 percent. Notice what happens if the price of the bond increases from $500 to $750. The return to the bond is now $250, because at maturity, the holder of the discount bond gets $1000, and he or she invested $750. As a result, the bondholder earned $250, or 33 percent of the initial investment. What is important to note is that as the price of the bond went up, i.e., from $500 to $750, the return went down, i.e., from $500 to $250, and the yield for the bond fell from 100 to 33 percent. That is, now a bank knows that the person buys the bond for $750 and gets $1000 at maturity, so the bank only has to pay 33 percent on the $750 deposit to give the person the same return as the bond and hence make them indifferent between buying the bond and depositing the money. This is a very important relationship; as the prices of bonds increase, the yield, or internal rates of return, to bonds decreases. Bond prices and yields (i.e., interest rates) are like children sitting on opposite ends of a seesaw. As one rises, the other falls.

The second kind of bond is the *fixed-rate bond*. The best way to think of this bond is as if it were a car payment or mortgage payment. The buyer of the bond receives a fixed payment every year after paying the initial bond price. This kind of bond is similar to an annuity that one may purchase on retirement, where one receives payments for the rest of one's life after trading in a large sum of money initially. From the perspective of the seller of the bond, it is the same as a car loan, where the bank loans an individual an initial amount, and the individual makes fixed payments every month for the next 5 years.

Fixed-rate bonds are similar to the third type of bond, which is called the *coupon bond*. The buyer of a coupon bond receives a fixed payment every year and, at the end of the maturity period, receives the face value of the bond. Thus, for example, if one buys a 30-year bond with a face value of $1000 and a coupon rate of 10 percent, the bond pays $100 a year for the next 30 years, and on the thirtieth year, the bond also pays the face value, or $1000. The only difference between a fixed-rate bond and a coupon bond is that the coupon bond makes the additional payment of its face value at the maturity date. If this were a loan, an example would be borrowing $20,000 for a car and paying the bank $100 a month for the next 5 years and on the last month paying the bank the usual $100 for that month as well as the $20,000 that was borrowed initially.

There are two subtle but important points to note about these bonds. The first is that *the yield is not equal to the coupon rate*. That is, in the example above, the $1000 face-value bond with a $100 coupon payment does not usually have a 10 percent yield. Remember that the yield is the interest rate that would make a person indifferent between depositing the amount of the bond price in the bank and buying the bond. The reason the yield is not 10 percent is because we have not specified what the bond price is. Because the yield represents the rate of return on the money invested in the bond, it is the interest rate of the bond, or the price the issuer of the bond has to pay to get the money from the bondholder. The bond is an IOU that promises to pay $100 for the next 30 years and $1000 on the thirtieth year. Suppose that General Motors issues the IOU. When someone buys the bond for, say, $500, GM receives $500 and pays $100 for the next 30 years and $1000 on the thirtieth year. Now suppose that the price of the bond, i.e., the IOU, increases to $750. Now GM receives $750 and *still pays the same amount* (100 for the next 30 years and $1000 on the thirtieth year). If we think that the interest rate is the coupon rate, which is 10 percent, we are saying that GM is paying 10 percent when it receives $500 and 10 percent when it receives $750. But how can it be paying 10 percent on two different amounts when it is making exactly the same payment in both cases? The answer is that GM is not paying 10 percent on the initial amount; it is paying a 10 percent coupon rate. From the point of view of the investor, what matters is the yield, which is the effective interest rate, or the internal rate of return on the investment. Obviously, if you are buying the IOU and you know that you are going to receive the same amount of money whether you pay $500 or $750, you would prefer to pay $500. In fact, the yield reflects this. The yield for the bond when the price is \$500 is about 20 percent, whereas the yield when the price is \$750 falls to 13 percent. Thus at the lower price you have the higher yield.

Now the question is, Where did the yields come from? Well, the answer to how to find the yield exactly is a tedious digression, and there is a simpler way to get a very close approximation of the yield. If we take the coupon payment on the bond and divide it by the price, we get the approximate yield. While this is not the exact yield to maturity, it is a good approximation, called the *current yield:*

$$\text{Current yield } i \approx \text{coupon payment/bond price}$$

If we do the math, \$100/\$750 $\approx$ 0.13 and \$100/\$500 $\approx$ 0.2. This is why yields and bond prices move in opposite directions. As the bond price gets bigger, the yield falls, and the reason is that the investment in the bond is less attractive (hence the lower yield) the bigger the bond price because the investor has to pay more but gets the same coupon payments and face value. Thus, as bond prices increase, yields on bonds fall.

The yields of the 30-year and 10-year Treasury Bonds are very closely watched interest rates in the economy. Nightly financial news programs always report them because they are an indicator of how the economy is doing. Inflation, for example, is a factor that can affect bond yields. Inflation is the yearly rate of increase in prices in the economy. Thus, for example, if prices double in one year, the inflation rate for that year will be 100 percent, because prices increased by 100 percent that year. If investors feel that inflation will increase in the future, they will abandon bonds. As investors sell bonds, bond prices will fall. As bond prices fall, the yield to bonds will increase. The reason investors do not like bonds during high inflation periods is that the payments made by bonds are fixed, so if inflation increases, investors are getting the same amount of money from bonds, while all the prices in the economy are rising. In order to induce people to hold bonds during higher inflation periods, the yield must rise, which implies that the price must fall, and this is what occurs.

If, for example, there is a lot of uncertainty and turbulence in the stock market, investors will run to bonds for shelter. The reason is that as stocks become riskier, bonds become more attractive because there is less relative risk of default for bonds. The bonds issued by the U.S. government, for example, are considered risk-free. As a result, there is no chance of default, which means that there is no risk that an investor will lose money when buying U.S. Treasury Bonds. As alternative investments become riskier, investors prefer to hold less of the risky investments and buy more bonds. As a result, the price of bonds increases during turbulent times, and the yield falls.

Now that you understand what the yield is, the question becomes, How is it relevant to the average small investor's decision? The answer is that the small investor must participate in a financial system that exists to facilitate many different sizes and kinds of investments. The changes driving the markets can be big investors driving large sums of money from one part of the financial system to the other in the hopes of hedging and protecting their wealth. A small investor attempting to participate in this market without knowing some of the major catalysts that cause shifts in the big money from one place to another, will be the last one to react, and thus will lose a lot of money.

The debt market, which is the bond market, is one of the major markets of the financial system, and the yields that are determined in these markets are the prices that move companies. The yields, or interest rates, give companies and corporations the incentives to invest and grow or to contract and lay off workers. While the stock markets may be more popular in the mind of the public and more widely followed, the debt markets are much bigger than the stock markets. Companies turn to selling debt and borrowing through bonds much more than through issuing stocks. Furthermore, in the stock markets, the buying and selling pressures determine the stock prices, but in the bond markets, the buying and selling determine the interest rate, which is the price of money, as we have seen. As a result, the outcome of trading on the debt markets affects everyone, not just those who are investing in bonds; the interest rates that emerge from the bond markets affect the interest rates on mortgages or car payments and can make paying for things in everyday life, such as a college education, more affordable because, for example, student loans may have lower interest rates.

Generally speaking, the debt markets and the equity markets can be thought of in the following simple fashion: Debt market participants are individuals and institutions who are involved in buying and selling loans and bonds. Equity market participants are individuals and institutions involved in the buying and selling of stocks, or ownership in companies, in the equities markets. There are other markets that make up part of the financial system as a whole, such as the market for money from other parts of the world, such as British money (i.e., the British pound). This market, the market where the dollar trades against money and currencies from around the world, is called the *foreign exchange market*. The foreign exchange market is important because it determines the exchange rate, which is the price of a U.S. dollar in terms of foreign currency. That is, the exchange rate is the price of a dollar in British pounds, for example, or in Mexican pesos, Canadian dollars, or Korean won. It is how many Mexican pesos you have to pay to get one U.S. dollar. Of course, one can invert the relationship and call the exchange rate how many dollars one has to give up to buy one Mexican peso. In doing so, one exchange rate just becomes the inverse of the other. Thus, for example, if it takes three Mexican pesos to buy one U.S. dollar, the exchange rate is 3. Equivalently, one can say that the price of one Mexican peso in dollar terms is 0.33, or 33 cents. In this case, one could say that the exchange rate is ⅓, because one-third of one dollar buys one Mexican peso. But this is equivalent to saying that three Mexican pesos buy one U.S. dollar. The fundamental idea is that the exchange rate can affect the prospects of a small investor because it can affect the profitability of many companies that are involved in global trade. For example, if the exchange rate is three Mexican pesos for one dollar, i.e., three to one, and the dollar gets more expensive in terms of Mexican pesos, we say that the exchange rate has appreciated and that the dollar is stronger. Suppose that the dollar appreciates from an exchange rate of 3 to an exchange rate of 4. Thus the exchange rate is now four Mexican pesos for one dollar. After the appreciation, the Mexican peso is less valuable in terms of dollars. Suppose that a company such as Caterpillar had plans to sell tractors to Mexico. If each one of the tractors cost $100,000 before the depreciation of the Mexican peso (and the corresponding appreciation of the U.S. dollar), the $100,000 tractor price would represent 300,000 Mexican pesos for a Mexican buyer. After the appreciation of the dollar (and the corresponding depreciation of the peso), the tractor price would increase to 400,000 Mexican pesos for the Mexican buyer. The situation is detrimental for both the Mexican buyer of the tractor, who can no longer afford to buy as many tractors as before, and the American company, in this case Caterpillar, because it loses sales. The tractor has become more expensive for the Mexican buyer, even though it is the same tractor, selling at the same price, with no changes or increased revenue for Caterpillar. The reason the tractor is more expensive is that the Mexican buyer must first buy dollars with Mexican pesos and then use those dollars to buy the tractor. If dollars are more expensive, then from the perspective of the Mexican buyer, the tractor is more expensive. This type of foreign exchange movement can hurt American companies that export and can make imports less expensive in the United States, hurting the competitiveness of domestic products. For example, if the dollar gets stronger relative to the Japanese yen, this means that one dollar now buys more yen than it used to. Thus a stronger dollar buys more Japanese currency than it used to. As a result, one dollar now buys more of anything that is paid for in Japanese yen. One item that is paid for in Japanese yen is a Japanese car. When one goes to an automobile dealership and buys a car that was built in Japan, one pays in dollars. The supplier of the car to the dealership, i.e., the person or company working on the docks that brought the car off the ship into the United States, however, had to pay the Japanese producer in yen. Hence, even though one pays in dollars, the price is just a reflection of the yen price that was paid further up the line, in the process of getting the car from Japan to the showroom in the United States. Hence, when the dollar gets stronger, it can hurt American car producers who compete with Japanese car producers. The flip side, however, is that Americans who import intermediate products from Japan, which are used to build their final products, such as computer makers who may import certain computer chips or components from Japan, are actually better off with a stronger dollar. For them it is cheaper to import the materials and intermediate products to build computers, so they are better off when the dollar appreciates. Hence the price of the dollar can affect the revenues that companies make, as well as their resulting stock prices.

The dollar price can further induce more important movements in the economy than just increased or decreased exports and imports. As the dollar gets stronger or weaker, people have an incentive to go and invest in other parts of the world. That is, as the dollar gets stronger and one U.S. dollar can buy more Japanese yen, one U.S. dollar also can buy more Japanese government bonds. As a result, an appreciation of the dollar is the same as if the price of Japanese government bonds fell. And as we have seen previously, as the price of a bond falls, the return to holding it, or the yield, increases. As a result, a stronger U.S. dollar can drive investors to invest in other parts of the world because for the same amount of money the American investor can buy more Japanese bonds than U.S. bonds. Hence the American investor can make a larger total return in Japan. As long as investors feel that they can get their money out of Japan at a reasonable exchange rate in the future, they will buy Japanese bonds today and invest in Japan rather than the United States. This is important because capital markets respond much more quickly than goods markets. That is, if the dollar gets stronger, it takes weeks to appreciate an increase in the amount of imports sold in the United States. If the dollar gets stronger and there is an increase in the return to investing in Japan relative to the return in investing in the United States, the participants and investors of the financial system know that they can send their money to Japan with one phone call or push of a button on a keyboard. As a result, the financial markets react very quickly to perceived changes in the relative return to investing in two different currencies due to changing exchange rates. As money is rushing around the international financial system, this too can affect stock prices, and the return to the small investor, as big investors pull out of Wall Street to invest in Japanese stocks, for example.

As far as the individuals actually transacting in these markets, whether they be equity markets, debt markets, foreign exchange markets, or some derivative markets, their basic function is to solve the problem of getting funds from lenders to borrowers. Generally speaking, there are two ways of doing this type of activity in financial markets, directly and indirectly. *Direct finance* occurs when, for example, one individual saves money and lends it to another for a business. In this way, the business is funded by a loan, and there is no third party intermediating the process of getting the money from the person who saved it to the person running the business. *Indirect finance* works the opposite way. In the case of indirect financing, the same business takes out a loan from a bank. The bank loans the business the money from the deposit account of the individual who saved up the money. Obviously, the bank takes a profit in that it charges the business a higher interest rate on the loan than it pays the depositor of the money. The bank is able to make this profit because of the problems that can arise when direct financing takes place.

One can imagine having saved up a large sum of money and then having to turn to investing it in a business run by someone else—how carefully scrutinized the business would be by the investor. The idea is that the person who saved the money has tied the money up in the business and would not want to see the business fail. This individual would watch the business very closely. By depositing the money in the bank, the person no longer has to worry about the business failing and the loss of savings. That problem is now in the hands of the bank. The money deposited in the bank will earn the interest promised by the bank with virtual certainty because the government insures deposits.

This simple example shows the important role played by financial intermediaries. Some of the most prosperous businesses in the economy are banks, investment firms, and other entities involved in the financial system as intermediaries. They make their money precisely by creating a value for their services by attempting to make it more attractive to the average investor to invest through their intermediation services rather than directly. The reason they can earn high rates of return on their intermediation and be successful in luring people to invest through them is because of the prevalence of three major problems in the financial system, as in almost all economic transactions. Economists call them *moral hazard, adverse selection,* and *transaction costs.*

The first of the three problems is *moral hazard.* This is the problem of not being able to see what someone else is doing after signing a contract. That is, one person who signed a contract knows more about what is going on than the opposite party who signed the contract. As a result, the person with whom one signs a contract can abuse the terms of the contract later. For example, suppose that you were to rent an apartment, and the landlord agrees that the cost of the utilities for the apartment are included in the rent. Then you could live in the apartment and use up lots of hot water and air conditioning and turn the heat way up in the winter because you do not care about the utilities bill because it is included in the rent. This could be described as a case of moral hazard because a landlord who knew that you were abusing the utilities in such a way probably would prefer not to pay for the utilities (although the smart landlord would assume that the utilities would be spent in this way and raise the rent accordingly, leaving you no choice but to use up lots of hot water and so on). Another extreme example of moral hazard would be someone taking out a fire insurance policy on his or her house and then burning it down just to collect the insurance money. Here the insurance company signs the contract to insure the property but then cannot watch the property all the time to make sure that no one is burning it down on purpose (for this type of moral hazard, insurance companies have arson investigators).

Moral hazard problems are prevalent in the financial system. In the example of the person saving up and investing in a small business, the investor must watch the business like a hawk after the money is invested. If not, the business partners running the business may take unnecessary risks or do less work than they should because they know they are not being watched. Financial intermediaries have a number of ways of dealing with moral hazard problems. For example, banks, when they lend, build long-term lending relationships with their customers. In this way the bank gets to know the person it is lending to, and the bank can see what types of risks exist and how the individual works. Furthermore, banks collect large amounts of information on the people who are borrowing from them, as well as on the types of businesses they are borrowing to start. In this way the bank gets a clear picture of how the businesses should perform and what to expect. The bank may require the person borrowing money to keep an account with the bank so that it can monitor how the individual spends money. The bank may monitor the borrower, audit the business balance sheet, and so on. All these are ways that the bank tries to get a clearer picture of what the person borrowing the money is doing once the individual has the money and no one is watching. This type of monitoring activity may be very expensive for an individual to do in terms of money, time, and expertise, so in this way the bank attempts to create value for the investor by lending and paying depositors for their investment dollars.

The second problem is *adverse selection.* Adverse selection deals with two parties signing a contract and one party knowing more about what is going on before the contract is signed than the other. Thus, for example, two people agree to something, but one person knows more about what they are agreeing to than the other. The person who knows less is aware of being at a disadvantage, and therefore will be willing to pay less. As a result, only people who are willing to accept contracts of lower value will sign. The classic example of adverse selection is the example of the used car market, which was pointed out by a famous economist named George Akerlof. Akerlof argued that when selling a used car, the seller knows more about the car than the buyer. As a result, the buyer will be wary of whether the car is in good condition, and knows that the seller has no incentive to reveal whether the car is in bad condition or not. Now, a buyer who knows that some used cars are in good condition, and some are in bad condition may lower the price to the condition of the average car. However, when the buyer does this, all the sellers who know that their cars are better than the average car will refuse to sell their cars for an average price (the price of the average car). Thus, a buyer who is willing to pay the average price will only buy from people who have cars worth as much as the buyer is willing to pay or less. That is, no one with a car worth more than the average price will sell to the individual looking to pay only the average price, whereas someone with a car worth less than the average price would gladly sell for the average price. And this is where the name comes from. This problem is called *adverse selection* because only the worst of the bunch stays. In this case, the people with the worse cars will be the most eager to sell at the average price because they stand to gain the most, since the car they are selling is the worst of the bunch. Another example of adverse selection can be health insurance companies. They know that health insurance premiums are expensive. As a result, someone who is most likely not going to get sick will prefer not to pay them. For example, young people do not need to worry about getting sick as much, so they may not want to pay high premiums for health insurance. People who are very likely to get sick and need to visit the doctor or buy medicine, however, will most likely want health insurance. These are people who know that they will need health insurance to pay for their hospital visits, so they do not mind paying the premiums. As a result, the health insurance company knows that the pool of applicants for its policy is, more likely than not, made up of people who think they may need health insurance rather than people who think they will most likely never use it. Again, this is adverse selection for the health insurance company. The company does not know as much about the person's physical condition as the person does himself or herself and, as a result, does not know as much about the future potential for medical costs.

The third way that financial intermediaries add value to a company is through economizing on transaction costs. *Transaction costs* are just the regular costs of doing business and getting things done. In the financial system, intermediaries can make it more profitable for the average person to use their services, rather than to engage directly in financing projects on their own and having to pay these costs. Some examples of transaction costs can be costs of keeping records, the costs of keeping cash safe, the costs of running credit checks, the costs of having borrowers in many different geographic locations, and so on. For example, it would obviously make more sense for a bank to handle keeping cash safe for many people than for many people to individually try to secure their life savings in their homes. The bank can economize and pay for one large vault, which would make more sense than for individual people to try to buy small safes to keep in their homes. It is this type of savings that enables banks to add value to the financial system.

This chapter has presented a brief overview of financial systems and some of the overarching issues with which we will deal. Some of the main issues are the postcontractual and precontractual differences in information, which are adverse selection and moral hazard. Financial intermediaries help abate these problems and help reduce transaction costs for participants of financial markets. We looked at some of the main sectors of the financial system, including the bond and foreign exchange markets. Finally, we looked at interest rates and yields, how they move, and why they concern so many investors and have such a strong influence in the economy. The next chapter looks at the features of the markets that we are interested in, which are the stock markets.

INVESTING—
THE BASICS

A recent book by Edward Chancellor[1] describes the proliferation of speculative activity throughout the history of financial markets. Speculative activity requires uncertainty, disagreement about unfolding future events, and a medium through which economic agents with different expectations can wager against each other. The uncertainty about the future has been a constant throughout history, as have the differences of opinion about this uncertainty. Insofar as a financial market has existed with sufficient depth and liquidity, speculation has existed alongside it.

[1] Edward Chancellor, *Devil Take the Hindmost: A History of Financial Speculation.* San Francisco: Farrar, Strauss & Giroux, 1999.

The speculative markets of today are no different from those of the past. We are in an economic expansion and a skyrocketing (so far) stock market,[2] the likes of which has never been seen in the history of the United States. The current economic expansion has led to a surge in asset prices and a bull market whose origins date back to 1991. Some individuals point to what Chairman of the Federal Reserve Alan Greenspan has called "irrational exuberance" as leading to asset price bubbles. An *asset price bubble* occurs when the price of an asset, such as a stock, is higher than its fundamental value and continues to go higher still because of speculative buying. These bubbles can lead to large corrections, sharp recessions, and in some cases even financial crises. If and when such a drastic pullback should occur remains to be seen. Surely the naysayers will be somewhat vindicated, since there are always market corrections. I am reminded, however, of a lesson that is diffused throughout the profession about the tulip mania that occurred in Holland in 1634. The price of tulips began to increase dramatically, and as more people began growing and trading them, they gained extraordinary value. The value of a tulip was high initially because many people wanted to own the tulips, and there were not enough to go around. Eventually, however, there came a point when the majority of the buyers of tulips were looking to resell at a higher price. Once this occurs, it is only a question of time before the price climbs so high that no one believes that it can possibly go any higher, and people stop buying the product. When this occurred, a huge sell-off ensued. This is referred to as the "bubble bursting." Many people lost the fortunes they had invested in tulips. The lesson is that although a tulip is only a flower, a rational individual will pay an outrageous amount for it if that person believes that it can be sold for more than the price paid. In all markets where speculative activity can occur, there are substantial profits to be made for those willing to bear the risks. Furthermore, the risk of investing in the stock market is not necessarily due to the fact that there is a bubble. It would be difficult to make the case that the historical behavior of the stock market is nothing more than a recurrent cycle of bubbles followed by financial crashes. If this were the case, an endless pool of speculators would be making and losing their fortunes as the market gyrates, year after year, in a string of boom and

---

[2] Keeping in mind that the stock market is much higher than 5 years ago; however, at each revision of this chapter, the issue of whether the stock market is rising given the current market behavior, was revisited.

bust cycles. Furthermore, stock prices would be dramatically unstable. This is not the case for the history of the U.S. stock markets. Moreover, the direct access trader will be among the most able of the market participants to protect his or her wealth in the event of a massive sell-off.

Say, for example, that the markets were in a bubble, and a massive sell-off ensued. Direct access trading systems are computerized trading systems now available to small investors based on recent technological advances. These advances give small investors access to the best information about the market and the ability to buy and sell instantly at the best prices from their personal computers. In such a situation, small investors without direct access would learn of the massive sell-off through financial television programs or their online brokers' Web pages. They would see delayed stock quotes, whereas the direct access traders would have real-time information on the market, as it occurs. The online traders may attempt to sell but would be at the end of the line, whereas direct access traders already would have liquidated their positions as they caught wind of the sell-off frenzy. In fact, by the time the small investor using an online broker scrambles to get what is available in the falling market, the direct access trader would have had ample opportunity to sell. Direct access would allow the trader to hold back until the markets level out and then buy back shares at rock-bottom prices. After a massive sell-off such as the one described, the markets settle into a period of uncertainty, like a mob without a leader. Direct access will allow the small investor to get in on opportunities, with the security of knowing that a quick exit is available. And this, of course, is not the normal market situation. Usually stock market movements are small, and stock prices remain relatively stable throughout trading. In this environment, the direct access trader can employ advances in information and access to markets to improve overall investments. With better information, the investment decision will be based on a clearer picture of the market and not on smoke and mirrors.

The story of the evolution of investing is one that is worth repeating at this point. It is often told in undergraduate economics classes. As this folk story goes, people decided that they had had enough of the bartering (e.g., trading apples for oranges) and invented money. As metallic coins began to appear, for security reasons people asked the village goldsmith to hold on to their coins for them. The smart goldsmiths realized that a large stock of money sat unused in their safes most of the time. These goldsmiths then began to loan out a part of the money people had given them to hold on to and charged interest to those who borrowed it. Today, the basic principle remains the same. We use complicated financial contracts and securities and employ the most advanced technology, but in the end it is all to get money from those who have it saved to those who need it to employ productive resources.

All the efforts expended to put borrowers and lenders together are not in vain. In a perfect world we would know exactly which businesses should be funded and what their profits will be, and everyone would have access to the same information. In this fantasy world we would be able to write contracts that would include all the possible outcomes so that there would be no surprises. Risk would be priced perfectly. A situation such as the one I am describing would consist of a completely frictionless capital market where there would be very little trading every day, and prices would almost never move. They would adjust instantaneously to any new information, as would market participants.

This, of course, is not reality. The fact of the matter is that as market participants try to match savings with borrowers, they face a myriad of problems due to misinformation and uncertainty. These problems are so acute that, in the past, most small investors sought a stockbroker to help them decide how to participate in the financial markets. Thus the broker has played the traditional role of mediator between borrowers and lenders in financial markets. That is, the stockbroker's traditional job in the market is to help people choose the right investments for their money. In theory, since a stockbroker works in the markets all day and small investors have other jobs, the broker should be ideal in helping the small investor secure the highest return possible. Unfortunately, stockbrokers have exploited this role of mediator tremendously. They have lowered the take-home returns significantly for small investors. They have exploited small investors to such an extent that the small investors have had to seek other means to participate in the stock markets. Many turned to online investing, for example. Now, because of advances in technology and the deregulation of markets, stockbrokers are no longer the only option or even the best for the vast majority of investors.

When investing in the market, we generally see that people fall into three categories:

- Those who invest through a broker
- Those who buy into a mutual fund
- Those who manage their own portfolio

THE BROKER

These days the use of a broker to invest has come under intense criticism, and not entirely without reason. As we shall see, stockbrokers face significant conflicts of interests when managing the money of small investors, and this is something that all interested parties should be aware of. Suppose you were to hire a stockbroker to handle your savings and suggest companies to buy into. Keep in mind that stockbrokers are employees of large brokerage firms. They work not just to serve your interests as a small client. They also work to serve the interests of the firms that employ them (i.e., the larger clients of the firm), as well as their own personal interests. These competing interests imply that the brokers' first priority may not always be to serve the small clients' best interests. You, as a small investor, may find yourself the lowest on the totem pole when it comes to stockbrokers.

We can think of the basic situation involving the investment process through the broker as follows: You, the client, show up with money to invest. At this point, you employ the services of a professional, much the same way as you would hire a lawyer to litigate a lawsuit for you or hire an agent to handle your career as a movie star. The basic difference is that the lawyer's and the agent's interests are aligned with yours. This is a very important difference, because it affects what counts most, the bottom line. If you collect a large settlement from your lawsuit, the lawyer's percentage gets larger. The lawyer makes more money as you make more money, so the lawyer will fight to get you every penny possible. Analogously, if your career takes off as a movie star, the agent makes more money as well. The funny thing is that payment to brokers is not directly related to the success of your portfolio. You can go broke or break the bank, and they get the same commission either way. In fact, they get more money based on more trading; i.e., they charge you more commissions the more you buy and sell. This gives rise to an obvious conflict of interest, in that the broker makes more money as you place more orders, regardless of whether the orders are terrible investments or not. Imagine if a broker offered to take 10 percent of the return on the portfolio the broker suggests for clients, for example. Of course, if the portfolio lost money, the broker would have to reimburse the clients 10 percent of the loss as well. This type of arrangement would benefit a broker who dispensed reliable investment advice. In such a case, the broker naturally would benefit from your success, in that the higher your portfolio went, the higher the broker's 10 percent would go. The world of imagination is the only place such brokers exist. And the important point is that the worst that could happen to a broker who fails to perform for you is the loss of your business as a client, a small client.

Now add to this the other interests of the broker. This individual may work for a large firm with clients much larger than you. While we may give the firm the benefit of the doubt insofar as it is likely looking to satisfy all its customers, certainly it would be naïve to think that the firm's top priority is anything but to satisfy its biggest clients. These large clients are the ones that generate revenue through huge commissions. If the firm's top priority is to make money, then its top priority boils down to keeping the big clients happy. Now consider the pool of employees working for the large brokerage firm. There are many stockbrokers, and naturally, some are more able than others. It is only logical to think that the most outstanding brokers handle the accounts of the big clients, not small individual investors. This means that you obviously are not receiving the services of the most qualified brokers on the firm's payroll. This makes sense for the firm, and it makes sense for the superstar brokers as well. Suppose you were a real mastermind at picking stocks. You could go nickel and dime a few small investors, you could handle multimillion-dollar accounts, or you could work for yourself. What would rational people do to serve their own best interests? In short, your broker may not be the most qualified person to handle your account. This fits in nicely with the fact that the broker's salary does not depend on the success of your portfolio, doesn't it?

Having said this, we should look at what does motivate the individual to whom you would hand over your hard-earned cash. The broker is part of a larger team, the brokerage house. These firms earn money by charging you a commission to sell your stock or buy stock for you on the markets. As we shall see, usually the firm has bought the stock at a lower price than the price it sold the stock to you or sold the stock at a higher price than you were paid for it.

There are two prices for each stock. One is called the *ask price,* or *the ask.* This is the price that people who currently own the stock and are supplying it to the market are asking for it. The second is the *bid price,* or *the bid.* This is the price that people who are demanding the stock are bidding to buy it. The bid is lower than the ask because if not, you could make infinite amounts of money by buying low and selling high. The difference between the bid and the ask is called *the spread*. For every stock, there are people corresponding to the buying and selling of the stock called *market makers* or *specialists*. The job of a market maker or a specialist is to ensure that there is always some stock for sale and always someone looking to buy a stock. With this, investors can always liquidate, or sell off, their positions in a stock. These market makers provide the liquidity, and they do it by buying and selling stocks. In exchange for this, they are allowed to charge a higher selling price than they pay to buy—this is why the bid is lower than the ask. The market makers will *always* buy low and sell high. These market makers work for the same brokerage houses that your stockbroker does. Suppose you call your broker and ask to buy a certain amount of stock. You pay the ask as your purchase price and, most likely, a commission as well. If the firm has a market maker in that stock, it pays the bid. If so, then it sold you a stock at the ask and made the spread. Additionally, in the time between when you decide to place an order and when the order is filled, the price can change. This change in price can cause you to lose money. For example, if you decide to buy a stock and then call your broker, who then puts the order in, by the time the stock is bought, the price may be higher. This waste of money is called *slippage*. As we shall see, direct access trading represents an immediate end to slippage.

Sometimes the firm does not have a market maker in the stock that you wish to purchase. That is, the firm does not have an employee who is responsible for providing liquidity in the stock that you are interested in buying. In this case, the broker calls a market maker and gives the market maker the order to buy. In return, that market maker gives the broker's firm a commission, called *payment for order flow*. It is illustrative to repeat this process. You ask to buy a stock, your broker gives your purchase to a market maker whom he or she has a previous arrangement with, and the broker gets a payment in return. How could an individual who represents a buyer get a payment from the seller? The mayor of the city I grew up in went to prison for doing this with construction contracts in city projects. Believe it or not, that is how things work. What is important to notice is that the broker generates money for the firm because the broker has access to the trading floor or to the market maker. A broker who did not have such access would not be able to make any money at all. With it, the broker makes the spreads for the firm, payment for order flow, and commissions every time you buy or sell stock.

MUTUAL FUNDS

Mutual funds (or other third-party institutions, such as pension funds) are institutions that pool the money of smaller investors together so as to have greater liquidity, better access to the market, better portfolio management, and so on. The idea behind a mutual fund is to economize on information-gathering costs and so on. It would not be feasible for the average small investor to pay a professional (of the mutual fund manager's caliber, not stockbrokers) or do the research himself or herself. If many people pool their money together, however, it becomes feasible. This is how a mutual fund works. The benefit of buying into a mutual fund is that you will have a staff of competent professionals handling the fund and hence your investment. They are rated on their performance and must actively compete with other mutual fund managers. They are constantly being analyzed by the financial press and are under a great deal of pressure to perform. Mutual fund managers generally do not face the blatant conflicts of interest that stockbrokers do. As a result of this competitive environment, mutual funds are fairly well managed. This type of investment is advisable for people who do not have as much time or interest to manage a portfolio of stocks or day trade. What's better, there are all kinds of mutual funds. One may invest in sector funds, such as the biotechnology sector, or high-technology stock mutual funds, aggressive growth or growth and income funds. There are many to choose from.

When looking at a mutual fund, it is helpful to see statistics that describe the performance of the mutual fund's portfolio. These are widely available and describe how the mutual fund managers have dealt with risk and what return they were able to generate in the past. These statistics are

Portfolio turnover. This statistic tells how much of the stock was sold, as a percentage of the stock owned by the mutual fund per year. An example would be if the portfolio turnover is 0 percent, it kept the same amount of stock and, therefore, sold no stock out of its portfolio. If the portfolio turnover is 100 percent, the mutual fund sold off all the stock it owned. Expenses for shareholders of the mutual fund (that's you) increase with turnover, since the fund has to pay more commissions. High turnover, however, is not necessarily bad if the trades are profitable.

R-squared (or R^2). This is the correlation coefficient between the portfolio of the mutual fund and the *market portfolio*. The market portfolio is a portfolio that represents a weighted average of all the stocks on the market. It is a big average of the entire market, and it represents the market performance in general. If the stock market were a classroom, the market portfolio would be the average grade, so to speak. One portfolio used to proxy the market portfolio is called the *S&P500*. The R^2 is a number between zero and one that represents how closely the mutual fund's portfolio shadows the market portfolio. If $R^2 = 1$, then the mutual fund's portfolio behaves exactly like the S&P500. This is important because the rising tide lifts all boats, as the expression goes, but some more than others. If the entire market is doing well, then portfolios with an $R^2 = 1$ will do well, and if the market falls, so will they.

Alpha. This statistic describes the performance of the fund given its risk level and the risk-free interest rate. If the alpha is positive, then the fund is doing better than expected for its risk level. If the alpha is negative, then the converse holds.

Beta. This is the risk coefficient of a fund in relation to the market portfolio. If the beta is 1, then the portfolio is as risky as the market portfolio. If the beta is 1.5, then the portfolio is 50 percent riskier than the market portfolio. If the beta is 0.77, then the portfolio is 23 percent less risky than the market portfolio.

Mutual funds charge fees and other expenses above and beyond the share price. These may be charged to pay administrative costs and so on. A front-loaded fund charges fees when you buy into the fund, and this can be a percentage of the share price, for example. A back-loaded fund charges fees when you sell out of the fund. A no-load fund does not charge fees when you buy into or sell out of the fund. Beyond these fees, the fund incurs expenses such as commissions and brokerage costs, which are passed on to the shareholders. There may be other charges as well, which are all laid out in detail in the fund prospectus.

Additional considerations that one should keep in mind with respect to mutual funds are, for example, the rate of return that results from the investment. Often mutual funds return less than the market portfolio, and beating it is considered good performance. This may seem like a low standard by which to measure success. The reason for this is that while mutual funds are well managed, the market portfolio is a weighted average of the market. This means that it accurately reflects what is going on and is not easy to beat. Using the preceding example, if we look at the stock market as a classroom, only half the children can be above average (i.e., the market portfolio), and the other half will be below average. Likewise, many managers often are not able to outperform the S&P500. Because of this, there are mutual funds that simply mimic the market portfolio; these are called *index funds*. These eliminate the manager's influence on the portfolio completely and ensure that the return will be the market return. Another concern is that part of the profits will be lost to taxes. Mutual funds face short-term capital gains taxes, which must be paid out by shareholders. Although individuals can lower their short-term capital gains taxes by holding on to stocks, this is not the case if you buy shares of a mutual fund. If the fund incurs short-term capital gains taxes and you buy in, part of your return will go to pay the taxes, whether you have held the stock for the entire year or not. The taxes are paid as they are levied. The costs of taxes are passed on to the shareholders as they are incurred, and if you hold shares in the mutual fund at that time, they will reduce your gains.

MANAGING YOUR OWN PORTFOLIO

Managing your own portfolio entails picking out stocks that you wish to own and buying them. With the advent of electronic access to the major stock markets, people can now call a broker or a discount broker to buy a stock. Investors can log on to an electronic broker or buy directly from a market maker or another investor on the Nasdaq through electronic direct access traders (more will be explained on all these options later). Electronic access allows for investing with very small commissions, and in the case of the Nasdaq, the instantaneous access opens the door for day trading, where individuals can trade like the market makers. Whether you are looking to hold on to stock in a company for months or just for a few minutes, electronic access has cut out the intermediary and made the purchase of securities more inexpensive. In managing your own portfolio, you may, for example, take a position in a company that you consider to be a good medium- to long-term investment. In this case, purchase of the stock through electronic direct access makes sense because of the savings in commissions and the ability to purchase at a lower price. If you are looking to day trade, forget about brokers. You need instantaneous access to markets. You cannot depend on the goodwill of a broker, clerk, market maker, or specialist to get your trade executed in the precious moments before the stock price changes or momentum swings against your position. The technology described in this book, called *electronic direct access trading,* is what makes this type of trading an option for small investors. It is this new technology and the deregulation of the markets that have improved the access for small investors.

These new possibilities for investment have broadened the set of choices available so that a small investor's only way into the markets is not just through expensive brokers, for example. Hence we have the three options available to put lenders and borrowers together on the stock markets. In order to decide which is right for you, it helps to know how money is made or lost on the stock market. In looking to make money in the stock market, investors hunt for bargains to buy and sell; hence investors must know something about how the market determines stock prices.

Business schools teach that a company's stock price *should* reflect the risk-adjusted net present value of its future earnings. This basically means that if you were to add up all the money that a company will make in the future (taking into account the likelihood of the company's success), subtract all its debts and costs, and divide by the number of shares outstanding, you would get the stock price. Thus what the stock price represents is a share of the future profits of the firm. The problem is that no one knows for sure what the future holds for a company. As technology progresses, some companies may become obsolete, whereas others may prosper. Some companies could be poorly managed or undercut by competition. Really, anything is possible. For this reason alone, the price of a stock shifts around. As new technologies develop and old ones become obsolete, people have to recalculate the net present value of a company's future earnings. Different analysts have different ideas about what a company is worth and hence what its stock price should be. Thus, even if we were to think that a stock price represents the future profits of a company, insofar as everyone cannot agree about the future profits of the company, they cannot agree about the stock price either.

Add to this the fact that not everyone has the same information about a company. At one extreme, some big institutional investors, such as mutual fund or pension fund managers, do tremendous amounts of research into companies. They have a staff of analysts researching companies' management strategies, as well as experts in every field looking at technological prospects. Market participants such as these know a lot about companies into which they buy. At the other extreme, however, scalpers and day traders look at minimal amounts of information on a particular company when deciding whether to buy into it. Hence it is not just disagreement about companies' prospects but also differences in what information is of interest to market participants that affect stock prices.

As market participants with different opinions about the stock price buy and sell throughout the day, the price is pushed up and down. Furthermore, new information spreads throughout the market unevenly. Suppose some people get information about a company ahead of others. They will be the first to the markets, and they will start pushing the price in a new direction, based on what they know. These information differences could lead to herding behavior, where most of the market participants follow a small group of market leaders just because it is assumed that the market leaders know more than the rest. All these buyers and sellers following each other around can make stock prices erratic. Finally, some market participants, including the scalpers mentioned earlier, out and out do not care at all about the prospects of a company. For some, the actual prospects of a company are of little interest because they may work with arbitrage relationships, such as programmed buying. Others may be readjusting their portfolios occasionally, selling to pay off debts, margin calls, and so on. Others yet may use limit orders to guard against a stock price moving the wrong way and sell or buy based on price movement itself rather than on some underlying information about the company. These are groups of market participants that when buying stock, do not care if a company is profitable or if it is going to go bankrupt in a week. They do not necessarily buy or sell stock because they think the company is great. They place orders to buy and sell because a stock price moved a certain way. In this case, stock price movement causes more stock price movement.

The reasons behind why individuals in the market buy and sell are as diverse as the individuals themselves. It should not be surprising to see stock prices moving up and down as buying and selling pressures shift. These movements in price, on the one hand, make the question of finding a profitable investment a nontrivial one but, on the other hand, create buying and selling opportunities with every movement. And in the end, this is how money is made in the stock market.

The question then becomes when to buy and when to sell with your savings. If you have absolutely no interest, and I mean no interest whatsoever, in investing, go with the stockbroker. The broker will minimize your involvement in the investment process, but be aware that your money will serve the interests of the broker and the broker's firm, the market maker or specialist representing the stocks the broker purchases for you, and finally, yourself. All these people make a living from your money, so make sure that the return to your investment is high enough to go around for everyone. If you have an interest in seeing your money invested wisely but simply do not have the time or interest to actively pursue particular stocks or to create your own portfolio, go with a mutual fund. Your investment will benefit from competent management and a competitive environment. In either of these alternatives, the decision of when to buy and when to sell has been handed to another party. The fundamental difference is that in the case of the mutual fund, you are aligning your interests with professionals who make their living investing. In the case of a broker, your interests will not necessarily be the highest priority to the broker.

If you want to keep the decision of when to buy and sell for yourself, then as an individual investor, you must decide whether to invest in a company for the long term, for a few months, for a few days, or to day trade. The fundamental difference is as follows: In the first case, sometimes called a *position trader,* you must research the companies yourself and decide which stocks to hold. In essence, you are competing with the mutual fund managers, and this is no walk in the park. This is not to say, however, that it is impossible to pick winners. With a conservative strategy, you can do well in the long run in the stock market as a position trader. In taking a position in a company, however, you are assuming the risks of that company. You are betting on that company's success over the term of your investment, and you are betting on that stock price increasing, taking into account all the market players and information effects. The benefits to this are that it is much more economical than using a broker and does not need to be a full-time job, unlike the opposite extreme, day trading. As a day trader, you take a position in a company and hold it for a very short amount of time. Having bought a stock, you sell it a few minutes later at a higher price and move on to another stock. As a result, you are not interested in the company fundamentals nearly as much as the other players. You only look to the price movement, hoping to anticipate its next move. The day trader assumes no long-run risk whatsoever. Whether the company fails or succeeds is irrelevant. What is relevant to the day trader is the short-run risk. The position trader and the day trader, like the momentum and swing traders, are simply working along different time horizons. Each assumes a different risk, and each must gather and process different kinds of information in order to be successful.

It is natural for the price of a stock to respond to the company fundamentals and to the relevant market information in the medium to long term. That is, a stock will in fact reflect the net present value of the company's future earnings in the long run because markets do not permit arbitrage opportunities in the long run (this is what the phrase "no free lunch" refers to). The medium to long run is the arena of position traders, so they must base their investments on the fundamentals of the companies in which they invest. They look to stock prices that will increase because the companies have become more profitable in the time they have held the stock. Position traders risk having to compete with players who have better access to information than they do about companies, as well as quicker access and better processing skills of the publicly available information on companies.

Alternatively, in the short run, the price of a company's stock can do almost anything. In fact, the stock price movement is modeled as a *martingale* in the short run by academics in finance and economics. This means that the best guess of where the price will be tomorrow is today's price. More precisely, the stock price surely will move, but it is so unpredictable that our best guess is that it will be worth tomorrow what it is worth today. This is the environment of a day trader. A day trader's job is to correctly anticipate the movement of a stock price and take the corresponding profitable position. The difficulty is that there is no easy or surefire way to do this. If there were, the profession would have ceased to exist, since price movements in stocks would be perfectly anticipated by day traders, and the market would be in constant equilibrium. The reason this does not happen is because people do not agree as to where the price is going and take opposite positions to one another. Hence, whenever one person is making money by selling a stock, the other person lost money in buying it. That is, if you buy a stock from me at a low price and sell it back to me at a higher price, the money you make equals the loss that I incur, and we both pay commissions.

To make money in the day trading or swing trading market, you have to anticipate the movements of stocks within a very short window of time. It takes full concentration, and it is a full-time job. The movement of a stock in the short run depends mainly on the response of the players involved in the market. This movement is nothing more than a reflection of the buying and selling pressures in the market for that stock. If more people want to buy than sell, the price increases. If more people want to sell than buy, the price falls. Thus we see that the day trader's job is nothing more than to anticipate the buying pressure and selling pressure. By learning the incentives and agendas of the different players in the short run, the day trader successfully anticipates the actions of the other players and positions himself or herself accordingly.

In the very short run, each market participant is essentially processing the same information. When considering the movement of a stock price in the last 5 minutes, none of the participants have time or, for that matter, use for information about the company fundamentals. Small bits of information are considered, but mainly what matters is who is in the game right now. Day traders look for information about who is looking to buy and how much. They also look for changes in the market sentiment, i.e., whether the general mood is optimistic, and buying pressures are present, or pessimistic, and selling pressures are present. Knowing these market tendencies is important because they can generate large price movements. If, for example, enough people think that the price of the stock will increase, they will buy it, and it increases. Then the participants may think that the price has gone too high and that they need to get out before it falls. By then it is too late, because everyone is thinking the same thing, so the price will fall as people rush to sell. These markets are subject to self-fulfilling prophecies. The job of the day trader is to move ahead of the market sentiment.

Long-term traders and day traders represent the two extreme time horizons, the long run and the short run. Traders who keep stocks for a few days or perhaps a few weeks are called *swing traders* and *momentum traders*. Knowing the characteristics of the long- and short-run markets helps these traders work through the medium run, when the markets make the transition from using short-run information to using long-run information.

As day traders have emerged in recent years, so in some circles have the criticisms of this type of speculating. The fact that markets are subject to the whims of investors bothers many people. This has always been the case, however; day traders did not initiate this at all. Furthermore, their rational self-interest contributes to keeping investors in line and the markets efficient. The role of day traders is not to finance successful investments; it is to provide liquidity to those investments. Thus, for example, people can buy into a company's stock and know that there is always an easy way out. There are always many active market participants willing to take the stock off their hands, including day traders. Being able to sell stock immediately and get money out of the markets is important because having to keep money tied up for long periods of time makes borrowing expensive. Imagine how much more difficult it would be for a company to sell stock if the stock could not be resold immediately. This problem does not exist because the markets are liquid, thanks in part to the daily trading activity of day traders and others. The fact that day traders are adding to the herding behavior of markets is a related line of criticism. This may be true, but this may be the price for having such a wide array of participants who add depth and liquidity to the markets. This makes the market more efficient, not less. It allows more financing of economic activity for the economy as a whole. Attempting to eliminate speculation and scalping in markets is a dangerous road to go down because it can lead to inefficient regulations. In the long run, investment in companies will decrease, and the economy will be worse off because of the inefficient regulations. The benefits of eliminating small investors and this kind of market participant through this type of regulation are not clear at all. All the problems that the regulation of speculative buying attempts to eliminate may persist.

Whether investing with a broker, a mutual fund, or as a small private investor, one should have at least a superficial understanding of the way stocks are classified in the market, how the markets are classified, and the jargon of market analysis. The most basic terms used to describe the markets and how they are performing are the bull and the bear. A *bull market* is an increasing market, where stock prices are steadily rising over time. A *bear market* is a falling and difficult market, where prices are decreasing.

We classify stocks according to how much the companies that are selling them are worth. This is called the *market capitalization* of the stock. *Market capitalization* describes how much a company's stock is worth because it is equal to the stock price multiplied by the total shares outstanding (total shares outstanding is abbreviated *TSO*). Thus, for example, if a company sells 1 million shares at $10 each, its market capitalization is $10 million. There are three main categories of market capitalization for stocks:

> *Large-cap stocks* are stocks with large capitalization. They are stocks of big companies with high stock prices and a large number of shares outstanding. Sometimes these companies are called *blue*

chips because traditionally the blue chips are the most expensive chips at the poker table. Blue chip companies are the cornerstones of the U.S. economy; they produce the products and services that are household names. They are, more often than not, leaders in their sectors. Blue chips represent a safer investment for the long term because they have proven track records and a good reputation.

Mid-cap stocks are stocks from companies that are smaller than blue chip companies but have stable track records and good growth potential. They are like smaller versions of large-cap stocks, and in their sectors, they do not have the clout of their large-cap counterparts. They represent slightly more risk than the blue chips and slightly more growth potential as well.

Small-cap stocks are the last category of market capitalization. These stocks are more inexpensive and have higher growth potential than the other two categories. They are usually from companies just starting out, with little or no track record. These companies are a more risky investment, and they tend to reinvest a higher portion of their revenues rather than pay out dividends. Small-cap companies are also more likely to pay out big if their companies succeed. In recent years, high-technology, biotech, and Internet start-ups have had very successful small-cap stocks.

Some small-cap companies are so small that their stock is not even traded on the small-cap market. These stocks are called *penny stocks* and are all sold over the counter. An *over-the-counter* market is simply a market where the stocks are not sold on an organized exchange, such as the New York Stock Exchange. Rather, in an over-the-counter market, transactions are conducted among dealers, brokers, and the public, off an organized exchange. Penny stocks are very risky investments. Their stock price is under $5, and they may have little or no history or a bad history. Penny stocks are not listed but are available through the Over-the-counter Bulletin Board (OTCBB).

All stocks fall into one of the classifications described above, but sometimes investors use classifications based on other characteristics of the stock beyond its market capitalization. A stock, like all assets, is valuable for two reasons. The first is how much income it pays to its owner, and the second is how much money its owner can make by reselling it. In technical terms, the resale profits are called *capital gains*. The income from owning the stock is called *instantaneous flow*. Capital gains depend on the price increasing after the stock is bought. The higher a stock's price goes after you buy it, the higher will be your capital gain, and the more valuable will be the stock. The instantaneous flow is the stream of dividends provided by the stock while you own it. This, in other words, is describing the money that the company pays to the owners of its stock. The higher are the dividends, the more valuable is the stock, because you will earn more money during the period of ownership. Stocks are often classified by the characteristics of their dividend stream and capital gains rather than their market capitalization.

One group of stocks, called *value stocks*, is based on capital gains. Stocks in this group are undervalued relative to how high their price will be in the near future. To identify value stocks, investors may look for growth potential, company changes such as restructuring, market price misalignments, or stock prices that are depressed by temporary declines in the economy.

Another group of stocks, called *income stocks*, has a high instantaneous flow, or a high dividend stream. Stocks in this group pay large dividends to their owners. These stocks are of interest to investors seeking to maximize income rather than capital gains. These investors are interested in capturing more of a company's period-by-period revenue and hence look for high-revenue companies that do not reinvest so much of their profits for growth but rather return them to the shareholders.

Some stocks have a dividend stream whose countercyclical timing is what sets them apart. These stocks are sometimes called *defensive stocks*. As the economy falters and a contraction or a recession sets in, most stocks pay out less. That is, when times are bad, normal companies are not making much money, so they do not pay as much revenue. Defensive stocks, however, do not decline in value because they naturally make money during hard times. Investors hedging against economic downturn may use stocks in this group.

The opposite of a defensive stock is a *cyclical stock*. These stocks do great when all is well and poorly when things are at their worst. They are like a fair-weather friend. Companies in these stocks prosper as the economy prospers and pull back with economic conditions as well.

The research done by analysts on Wall Street about companies is an integral part of the investment decision of all traders, whether you wish to invest for 10 seconds or 10 years. The publication of earnings reports and analyst recommendations move stock prices and have all sorts of effects on the markets (which are described in later chapters). In order to understand their effects, one must understand some basic language that these analysts throw around in their reports.

In the most general case, analysts issue a buy recommendation that falls into one of five categories. They are *strong buy, buy, hold, underperform,* and *sell.* These categories are listed in order of best to worst recommendation, the best being a strong buy recommendation and the worst being a sell recommendation. Thus, if an analyst report recommends a stock as a strong buy, for example, the report is giving that stock the best recommendation it can. Analysts also look at *earnings per share* (EPS). The EPS number captures the part of the company's revenue that is returned to the shareholders. Thus, for instance, after a company collects revenue from product sales, part of the revenue goes to paying its employees, and part goes into reinvesting in its plants and equipment. The rest of the revenue, i.e., the part that is not used for investment or for covering costs of production, is returned to the shareholders and is called *earnings.* Dividing the earnings returned to customers by the number of shares sold is how EPS is calculated. Intuitively, it is the amount of money that each share pays to its owner (recall that *total shares outstanding* is abbreviated TSO):

$$EPS = net\ income/TSO$$

The actual EPS for a company is preceded by the *forecast of earnings.* This is just the expected earnings for a company by Wall Street analysts. It is the best guess of the earnings that the company will generate. It can be forecasted quarterly or yearly, and the forecast is a kind of average of all the analysts' forecasts. This average is called a *consensus forecast.* Often published along with the consensus forecast are the highest and lowest forecasts and the number of up and down revisions from the previous forecasts. These revisions occur because between one forecast and another, news may break or new information may emerge about a company or the economy that may lead analysts to revise their forecasts.

Another statistic that appears in analyst reports is *earnings surprise.* Earnings surprise is just the difference between what analysts expected a company to earn per share (i.e., EPS) and what the company actually earned. Having established the consensus on how a company's EPS will turn out, the earnings surprise is calculated as the percent of the observed or actual EPS that was not expected by analysts. This statistic is available after a company releases its earnings.

$$ES = (consensus\ EPS - actual\ EPS)/consensus\ EPS$$

Momentum looks at how the analysts are viewing a company as a group. It is a chart that shows how analysts' feelings about a company are changing over time. Momentum measures how attractive or unattractive a stock is becoming to analysts. For example, a momentum chart may look at how consensus EPS has been changing over time. Momentum is looked at because while one analyst may be wrong about a company, it is difficult to believe that they are all wrong all the time about a company. Then, as a group, they can accurately predict how stocks will perform. As momentum changes, these changes may be early indicators of changes in future stock prices.

The *price-to-earnings ratio*, or *P/E ratio*, is another well-known indicator of a stock's performance. It is calculated as the stock price divided by the EPS. A low P/E ratio indicates that a company has high earnings relative to its market value, which makes it a good investment. The intuition is that the company is a good one to buy because it makes a lot of money but does not cost a lot.

$$P/E = \text{stock price}/EPS$$

Earnings growth is the predicted value of the EPS of the company, as the name suggests. Analysts combine the P/E ratio with earnings growth to construct a statistic called the *PEG*. The PEG is the P/E ratio divided by the expected growth rate. The lower the value of the PEG, the better is the expected future performance of the company.

$$PEG = P/E \text{ ratio}/\text{earnings growth}$$

All these statistics, PEG, P/E, EPS, etc., appear in analysts' reports on companies and are useful not only to predict the future of a company and its stock but also, more important, to predict the behavior of the market. The reports influence the market. In and of themselves, these reports can be as influential to the stock price of a company as the company's fundamentals and management.

In this chapter we have seen the alternatives available to individuals for investing. We have seen that stock markets naturally give rise to problems of information and uncertainty and the instruments available to every investor to address these problems when investing. The next chapter takes a closer look at the environment in which trading occurs on the market.

We will look at the types of stock markets and the types of buying and selling that occur on these markets.

QUESTIONS

1   What is the best way to use the normal analyst statistics on stocks, such as P/E ratios and earnings growth?

2   How relevant or irrelevant have the traditional statistics kept on stocks, such as P/E ratios, become, especially in light of the enormous bull market, in which we have seen very high numbers?

3   What types of stocks have good indicators, such as analyst reports, and what types of stocks tend to perform differently from analyst expectations?

4   Are small-cap stocks a good investment for the small investor? Are penny stocks?

5   What are the possibilities for the small investor in trading mutual funds?

4

THE MARKETS

In 1653, as the Dutch settled lower Manhattan, they erected a stockade to defend against attacks. It stretched across the island from one river to the other. Years later, in 1685, a street was laid out along the line of that stockade. It was appropriately named Wall Street, and the settlement developed into New York City. About a century later, after independence from the British, the first U.S. Secretary of the Treasury, Alexander Hamilton, sold $80 million of U.S. Revolutionary War debt. This war debt was the first type of security traded in New York. Under Hamilton's auspices, the first trading of these securities began to occur regularly on the corner of Wall Street and Broad Street. The present-day securities markets that arose from those beginnings are the work environment of the small investor and the subject of this chapter.

The securities markets that sell stocks, options, and so on can be organized in one of two different ways. The first type of organization is called an *auction market*, and the second type is called a *dealer-driven market*. While there are many auction markets, we will confine our interest to the biggest, the New York Stock Exchange (NYSE). As far as dealer-driven markets are concerned, we also will confine our interest to the biggest, which is the Nasdaq. The new electronic environment available to the small investor allows access to both types of markets, and it behooves all investors to know something about what it is that they are gaining access to. This chapter will take a closer look at these markets and present some of the basic features that are necessary for understanding how to navigate through them successfully. Many investors, at the beginning, are confused by complicated-sounding terminology used on the markets. We will clear up the confusion about a lot of the fancy words used by the professionals on Wall Street, which for the most part sound more complicated than they are. With these concepts, the workings of the markets are easy to understand. Now more than ever, the Nasdaq and the NYSE are available to everyone, and with some simple concepts, investing in them successfully can be easier than ever. While there are important differences in the two types of markets, before looking at these differences, it is helpful to look at the characteristics that they share.

These markets exist to facilitate the exchange of ownership in publicly traded companies. Either by explicit regulation or by convention, the way business is conducted on these exchanges adheres to a particular but fairly simple protocol. That is, traders and market participants speak and conduct themselves in a standard way so that they can all easily work with each other. In order to understand the trading that occurs on these exchanges, one must first understand the basics of the language of investing in these markets.

What is commonly known as the *stock market* is a collection of markets, one for each stock being traded. Hence we can think of the stock market as a group of many small markets for stocks. The first time a stock is sold is when a company sells its ownership rights to the public. This is called an *initial public offering* (IPO). The buying of IPO stock is called the *primary market*. Thus, for example, if a private company decides that it is going public, when the stock is first sold, it is called the primary market. This is an extremely lucrative market; the one-day gains of some of the technology IPOs are unbelievable. Unfortunately, this market is restricted to market participants who are considered *valued client status* (VCS) *customers* by the underwriting firm. These are customers with a lot of trading volume, such as institutional investors. Some examples of institutional investors are pension funds, mutual funds, insurance companies, and large brokerage firms. These customers are rewarded with IPOs because of the enormous commissions they generate to the underwriting firms through their sheer trade volume.

As soon as a stock bought through an IPO is resold, it is on the *secondary market*. This is where most of us operate. Roughly speaking, primary and secondary markets are analogous to new and used car markets. The example of new versus used cars should not lead one to think that stock on the secondary market is less valuable because used cars are less valuable than new cars. In this sense, stocks are more like paintings by Monet. They are valuable because of the artist, and the fact that they are preowned is irrelevant. What matters for stock is its current value and where the future value may be. What we know as the stock market is almost always considered secondary market trades.

Recall that each stock is traded within a market of its own. This market contains a price and quantity representing the demand for the issue and a corresponding price and quantity representing the supply for the issue. That is, what we call a market is how much stock there is for sale and at what price and how much stock people are interested in buying and at what price. In these markets there is an institution that is responsible for providing liquidity. In the case of the NYSE, an individual, called a *specialist*, represents this institution. On the Nasdaq, a group of individuals, called *market makers*, is collectively responsible for providing liquidity. To provide liquidity means that there must be both supply and demand represented on the market for each stock at all times. Thus, for example, if at some point no one is interested in buying a stock, these institutions must step up and buy from people who wish to sell. If there were no individuals looking to sell a stock, market makers or the specialist must sell from their inventories to those interested in buying the stock. This is what *providing liquidity* means. In exchange for this responsibility, the specialist or market makers are allowed to charge a higher sale price, i.e., supply price, than their buy price, i.e., demand price. Thus they sell at a higher price than they buy. In short, there are lots of markets, where we have twin prices and twin quantities describing the markets. These are the demand price and the quantity demanded at that price and the supply price and the corresponding quantity offered at that price. It all boils down to supply and demand.

The basic idea of buying low and selling high has an interesting variation, which is to sell high first and later buy low. This type of selling is called a *short sale*, or *selling a stock short*, or *taking the short position*. A short sale entails selling a stock that you do not yet own. When the price falls, you buy at the lower price the stock that you had previously sold at a higher price. The idea behind short selling is to find bargains across time. How it works is that your brokerage firm may have stock that belongs to someone else in its account, and you sell it. In this situation, you have borrowed the stock from the owner and sold it to someone. You then wait until the price falls and buy the stock back to replace it. When you buy back the stock at a lower price, you have made a profit. There are special rules for the short selling of stocks because it entails the selling of stock that belongs to someone else. Each market specifies its own rules, but the general idea behind them is that you cannot sell a stock short as its price is falling. The reason for this is that a large sell-off would ensue, causing markets to crash. The short-selling rules will be described along with each market.

The opposite of taking the short position is to *take the long position*. In this case, you are buying a stock at a low price so that when the price increases, you can sell it for a profit. This is the traditional buy low, sell high advice. It is called a *long sale*, or to *go long on a stock*.

The prices in these markets have names. The name of the demand price is the *bid*. The bid represents the price that market participants are bidding for a stock. If you need to sell something quickly, you may have to sell it on the bid, or get paid the bid for the sale. The name of the supply price is the *ask*, and this is also known as the *offer*. The offer is the price of stock for sale at the market. If you need to buy something quickly, you may buy it on the offer; this means that you buy the stock and pay the offer for the purchase. It is obviously more convenient to say "the bid" than "the demand price" and "the ask" than "the supply price." The bid is usually lower than the ask because market makers buy low and sell high. That is, they buy at the bid and sell at the ask. The bid and the ask are expressed in dollars and fractions of dollars. Presently, the lowest fraction of a dollar that can be traded is $1/16$, commonly referred to as a *teenie*. From there, stocks are traded at $1/8$, $1/4$, $1/2$, and so on. Thus, for example, a stock price of $50\frac{1}{2}$ means that the stock is selling for $50.50 per share. Each company has an abbreviation of up to five letters on the exchange. Thus, for example, the market for Motorola, Inc., which is abbreviated *MOT,* may be

MOT   148¹³⁄₁₆ × 148¹⁵⁄₁₆   1000 × 2000
STOCK SYMBOL   BID PRICE   ASK PRICE   BID SIZE   ASK SIZE

This example says that the market will pay 148¹³⁄₁₆ for 1000 shares of MOT that you may choose to sell. This is the bid and the quantity demanded at the bid. Remember that the market buys at the bid. The market is willing to sell you 2000 shares of MOT at 148¹⁵⁄₁₆. This is the ask, or offer, and the quantity supplied to the market at the ask. The difference between the bid and the ask is called the *spread*. In MOT's case, the spread is ⅛ point, which is the same as $0.125. Note that a dollar is equal to 1 point. Another important point to note is the way buying and selling is expressed. One says that one will *buy* at *price for size*. Thus, for example, you bid 20½ for 300 shares. Conversely, one says that one will *sell* a *size at price*. Thus you offer 300 shares for 20½. In the preceding example, it is correct to say that the market maker Bear Sterns, abbreviated *BEST*, bids 148¹³⁄₁₆ for 1000 shares of MOT but *incorrect* to say that BEST wants to buy 1000 shares at 148¹³⁄₁₆ from you. This would be confusing to someone because you are describing a sale but speaking in terms of an offer. The analogous example for an offer is to say that BEST is offering 2000 at 148¹⁵⁄₁₆, *not* that BEST is expecting to get 148¹⁵⁄₁₆ for the 2000 shares it is offering.

The market for stocks is constantly changing as demand and supply for the stock shift around throughout the trading day. The bid and the ask are moving up and down, depending on whether the demand is greater than the supply, or vice versa. Excess demand puts upward pressure on the bid and the ask, and excess supply puts downward pressure on them. Thus, if a market participant believes a stock is really hot and has to have it, he or she will demand it and may buy up all the stock offered. This will increase demand and reduce the supply of the stock, causing its bid and ask to increase. These movements in the stock price will occur in specific predetermined increments, called *levels*. Going back to the preceding example, the spread for MOT is ⅛, so its levels may be teenies, or ¹⁄₁₆. The levels are the size of the movements in the price as the price changes. This means that as MOT is slowly bid up, the market may move to

MOT   148⅞ × 149   1000 × 500

In this example, the bid and the ask moved up one level, and the offer size has fallen to 500 shares. The size of the incremental increase in the bid and ask is $\frac{1}{16}$; this is what the level refers to. The positive move in the stock price is referred to as an *uptick* or *upbid* depending on the market. On the NYSE, the increase in prices is called an *uptick*. On the Nasdaq, the increase in prices is called an *upbid*. If the market were to be quoted again and the bid stayed at 148⅞, this would be called a *zero-plus*. This means that the bid remained the same but that the last time it moved, it moved up. In the opposite case, if the bid were to decrease, this would be referred to as a *downtick*. If the bid were to stay the same, but the last movement was a decrease, this would be referred to as a *zero-minus*. Note that the description of the market bid, offer, and size is referred to as a *quote*. Additionally, when quoting a stock, bidding, or offering, traders sometimes refer to the *inside market*. This term refers to the price area between the bid and the ask. That is, the inside market refers to the highest buying price, or bid, and the lowest selling price, or ask. If you were to bid 148¹⁵⁄₁₆, you would be on the inside of the market because your bid is higher than the current bid; i.e., you would be the new highest bidder.

When bidding or offering, one does not necessarily have to hit the bid, lift the offer, or be on the inside of the market. There are many different ways to place buy and sell orders so as to take advantage not of where the stock is selling at now but of where its price may be headed. We now turn to the different ways to buy stock.

Market Orders. These are the normal orders that one would expect, where you see

$$\text{MOT} \qquad 148\tfrac{7}{8} \times 149 \qquad 1000 \times 500$$

On submitting a market order, the trader is attempting to purchase shares of MOT at the current offer, in this case 149. Hence a market order is nothing more than an attempt to buy or sell at the current bid or ask. A trader who wants to buy tries to buy on the offer. A trader who wants to sell tries to sell on the bid. The trader may not get the offer or the bid if the markets are very active and other traders beat him or her to it. That is, the stock that is available at the current market may be sold already by the time the trader puts in an order. Direct access is designed precisely to help the small investor get into the markets with greater speed so as to get the market orders quickly before the available stock is gone.

Limit Order. You place a limit order in the case where you do not want to buy or sell the stock until at least the price reaches a limit of your choosing. Your order is not filled unless the stock trades at the limit you chose or better. While you are not guaranteed that the order will be filled at your limit price, it will not be filled at a worse price. Additionally, limit orders are queued, so if your order is the next in line, it will be filled the moment the stock trades at your limit price. Suppose that you are interested in buying MOT, and the current market quote is

MOT   148⅞ × 149   1000 × 500

A limit order to buy with a limit price of 148¹⁵/₁₆ means that you will not buy until the offer comes down to 148¹⁵/₁₆. Once it does, you may get the order filled at that price. If you do not, it may be due to other limit orders that were queued ahead of you. The offer price may continue to fall, in which case your order may be filled at a better price (i.e., a lower offer price, so it is cheaper for you). If your order is not filled, it may be because the offer turned back up; i.e., it went back above 148¹⁵/₁₆ before your order was filled. If this occurs, your offer may not be filled until such time as it returns to 148¹⁵/₁₆. In the case that the stock price does not move in that direction, you may cancel the order yourself, or it may expire. In some cases, the order may not expire until as late as the end of the following month from the day you place the order. You should be aware of how long the order stays on the books. This is not difficult, however, because you can easily see your current and past orders on most types of trading screens.

Stop Order. A stop order is used to keep losses down. It is similar to a limit order in that your trade is filled if the stock price reaches or passes a certain point, called a *trigger price*. This type of order is used to exit a bad trade. As such, the trigger price must be below the bid in the case of a sale stop order and must be above the ask in the case of a buy stop order. Hence, while a limit order is used to take a position as the market moves in your favor, a stop order is used to exit a position as the market moves against you. As an example, consider the following market:

GE   123 × 123¼   1000 × 1000

Suppose that you lift the offer and pay 123¼ for 1000 shares of General Electric. The new market quote shows that the market moved in your favor. Now the quote is

GE   123¼ × 123½   1000 × 2000

If you paid 123¼ for 1000 shares of GE and sold at the bid in this market, you would break even (except for the round-trip commissions). If you think the stock may pull back, you may want to limit your losses on this trade to $250. That is, in the case that the price falls, you might want to sell before the fall is too great and you face a large loss. If GE falls ¼ of a point, you may need to get out. To be on the safe side, you may set a sell stop order with the trigger price at 123¹⁄₁₆. Here, what you are ordering is that your 1000 shares of GE be sold if the bid were to fall to or past 123¹⁄₁₆. In this way you only lose $187.50 plus commissions on the trade. The loss is calculated by taking the ³⁄₁₆ loss on each share (due to the bid price falling from 123¼ to 123¹⁄₁₆) and multiplying by the 1000 shares that you own. That is, you own 1000 shares that have fallen ³⁄₁₆ each, so the loss is ³⁄₁₆ × 1000. On top of this, of course, you lose commissions on the buy and the sell orders. You also may place a buy stop order, where the trigger price must be above the current ask price.

Stop Limit Order. As the name suggests, this order is a combination of a limit order and a stop order. It is like a stop order, in that you set a trigger price below the bid or above the ask. Thus, in this sense, a stop limit order is used to keep losses down. When the market price reaches the trigger price, that trigger price becomes the limit price of a limit order. This means that you are using a stop order to limit your losses, but you will not accept a price worse than the trigger price to fill your order. For this reason, when the trigger price is reached, you make it a limit order so that you cannot buy the stock at a price worse than that original trigger price. Looking at the example from above:

GE   123¼ × 123½   1000 × 2000

Recall that you set a buy stop order with a trigger price of 123¹⁄₁₆. Now, suppose that the order is a stop limit order. When the bid for GE falls to 123¹⁄₁₆, your order calls for the sale of 1000 shares of GE at 123¹⁄₁₆. If it is just a stop order and the bid continues to fall without your

1000 shares being sold, your order may be filled at a lower bid. However, with the stop limit order, the trigger price of 123¹⁄₁₆ becomes a limit price. You will not sell at 123 or lower, only at 123¹⁄₁₆ or higher. Recall that you bought the stock at 123¼, so your losses are being limited by the stop limit order.

In addition to the different buy/sell orders described above, you can restrict your orders in a number of ways. Some of these restrictions are as follows:

Good till cancelled (GTC). Your order is good until you cancel it. That is, the order expires when you cancel it only.

Day order (DAY). The order expires at the end of the trading day.

All or none (AON). This restriction is for trades of 300 or more shares, and it restricts the order to buy or sell only if the entire block of shares is available. If not, then the order is not filled.

Do not reduce (DNR). This restricts the order price from being reduced in the event of a stock split or dividend payout.

Fill or kill (FOK). Fill the entire order at the limit price given or better, or cancel it.

THE MARKETS

New York Stock Exchange

The New York Stock Exchange, abbreviated NYSE, is often referred to as the "big board." The stocks that sell on the NYSE are called *listed stocks*. This market, like the American Exchange and many others, is an auction market. In auction markets there is an actual physical place where the interested parties get together to trade stocks. There is an individual called a *specialist* who runs a double auction for the stock while it is traded. In the case of the NYSE, the place is the exchange on the corner of Wall Street and Broad Street in New York City. Trading on the stock begins when the specialist opens the market and depends exclusively on him or her actually showing up to work each morning.

The specialist looks at how much stock is demanded and how much is supplied and sets the market appropriately. The specialist announces the price and size for the stock, and has the obligation to keep a fair and orderly market. Additionally, the specialist must provide liquidity for the market. If there is a large buy order for the market, the specialist sells all the offered stock and then must sell stock out of his or her own personal inventory. Notice that the specialist has the advantageous position of being the last one to sell, when the supply of the stock has been exhausted, and the stock is scarcest. This scarcity enables the specialist to sell at the highest price. That is, when all the stock available is gone, then the specialist sells, and gets the highest price. Conversely, if there is a large sell order, the flood of stock will quickly drive down the price and exhaust the bids on the market. When all the current bids have been exhausted, the specialist begins to buy, to clean up the order. The specialist buys at a lower price than any of the other market participants because everyone interested in buying is gone.

The specialist is in an advantageous position for another important reason. The specialist, and only the specialist, is able to see the entire market flow. That is, the specialist can see how much everyone demands and how much everyone supplies, and for this reason, can buy and sell very easily at the troughs and peaks of the stock price movements.

The rules that govern trading on the exchange are:

1 First come, first serve at every price.

2 High bid and low offer have the floor.

3 For a new auction to begin, all the bids and offers at the current price must be exhausted.

4 No secret transactions are permitted.

5 The bids are to be made to the specialist in an audible voice.

6 The specialist controls the floor; trading depends on the specialist exclusively.

7 A 50-point drop halts trading on the issue, and the specialist can reopen the market at a different price.

8 *Short sale rule:* A short sale order may be executed only on a plus-tick or zero plus-tick.

Actual market participants on the NYSE double auction markets include the floor brokers representing different firms and the specialists. These are the people who stand around in the trading pits on the NYSE. In order to make a purchase on the exchange, the order must either go through a floor broker, or a *designated order turnaround system,* abbreviated *DOT.* This is a computer that was used in the past to send orders to the specialist on the NYSE. The DOT was replaced in 1984 by SuperDOT, which is just a bigger version, capable of handling more orders. SuperDOT is an electronic order delivery system, like a small intranet system. It is used by member firms to access the NYSE and only the NYSE. Through this system, an order can be sent to a specialist, who either places the order on his or her limit book or attempts to fill the order immediately. Confirmation of the order is then sent back to the member firm that placed the order. It is like emailing the specialist the order to buy or sell. This system handles the lion's share of orders placed on the NYSE. The largest orders, and hence the most share volume, is ordered through floor brokers, not SuperDOT. Brokers handle the most volume because for a large market participant, such as a pension fund, it is more economical to have a broker representing the fund's interests. Since a pension fund's orders can be quite large, the fund may prefer to pay a broker to look for the best price possible rather than to send a large order using SuperDOT and risk pushing the stock price against the fund itself.

The dependence on specialists for trading on the NYSE works against the electronic trader. The specialist is the only one who can see the entire market. If there is any imbalance in supply or demand of an asset, you can be sure that the specialist will take the beneficial position. Hence the specialist is better informed about the market than anyone else. Another disadvantage is that the NYSE has much less volatility in stock price movement. This is due in part to specialists absorbing excess demand or supply for themselves rather than allowing the markets to clear at higher or lower prices. Specialists can observe all the selling and buying pressure and know which way the price will move. Additionally, they do not even have to accurately represent this selling and buying pressure. Specialists can quote size and price in any way that they choose, so long as they are consistent with the orders in their limit order book. That is, as long as no one waiting to buy or sell is skipped, the specialist can change the market quotes as desired. The quote is the best information about the market available. It is naïve to think that the market quote represents the true selling and buying interest in a stock. Rather, it represents what the specialist would like people to believe is the demand and supply at the given prices. As long as the quote is honored, the specialist can quote anything desired, irrespective of what the aggregated market orders for a stock truly are.

Suppose, for example, that on a given day, the market for Pepsico is

PEP   34¼ × 34½   3000 × 4000

Suppose that a broker received an order to buy 25,000 shares of PEP at no more than 34¾. The broker may ask the specialist at what price the 25,000 shares can be bought. The specialist may tell the broker to buy 10,000 at 34½, another 10,000 at 34⅝, and the remaining 5000 at 34¾. At this point, the specialist knows that there is a large buy about to take place. As a result, the specialist can securely advertise large amounts of stock for sale so as to create the illusion that a sell-off has begun. In fact, it has not. It may simply be some large institutional client rebalancing its portfolio. If the specialist shows lots of stock for sale, some people in the market may perceive that the stock is getting weaker and try to get out. Then the specialist may show the new market immediately at

PEP   34¼ × 34½   3000 × 25,000

Here, the market suddenly has a lot of stock for sale. Many participants may mistakenly believe that the stock is on the way down and try to sell it. If so, they may lower their offers or even sell on the bid. In fact, the stock is on the way up. As the new sellers enter the market, the broker may buy up all the extra stock supplied and quote the market again at

PEP   34½ × 34¾   3000 × 5000

Here, the specialist has filled the broker's order from a personal inventory and limit orders on the book. The specialist sold the broker 10,000 at 34½, another 10,000 at 34⅝, and the remaining 5000 at 34¾. Meanwhile, the specialist has bought stock at or below 34½ the entire time. The specialist may have had some nervous traders hit the original 34¼ bid even. Remember that the specialist naturally sells into a rising market and buys into a falling market. The best a small trader can do is to trade with the specialist, and this is difficult to do because of the vast differences in information.

Further disadvantages for the small trader on the NYSE are the lack of volatility of the listed stocks. These are older, more stable companies, for whom a large movement is a 1-point move in a day. Furthermore, the specialist, rather than let the stock move around, makes profits of large buying and selling pressures, which further takes away from the stock price volatility. Volatility is good for the day trader. Day trading revolves around selling stock quickly and moving on to the next buying opportunity. If the price hardly moves or takes a long time to move on normal days, then it is no place for a day trader to make money.

Finally, the timing of the trades on the NYSE is not beneficial for day trading. If a day trader sends a specialist an order on SuperDOT, the specialist has 2 minutes to *attempt* to fill the order. This means that the trade may be filled much later and at a different price than when originally ordered by the day trader. The order, furthermore, is sitting on the books the whole time, while the market moves. Meanwhile, there are brokers on the trading floor representing the orders of their clients, who can look after these clients' interests. Your order will be handled within the regulations, but if the market moves against you and the volume of trade is high, you will be in a bad position.

The Nasdaq Markets

The National Association of Securities Dealers Automated Quotations National Market and Small-Cap Market comprise the other major stock market that is of concern to us. They are officially named the *Nasdaq National Market* and the *Nasdaq Small-Cap Market,* commonly known as the *Nasdaq.* It is also known as the *over-the-counter* (OTC) *market.*

The origins of the Nasdaq date back to a report submitted to Congress by the Securities and Exchange Commission (SEC) in 1963. The report characterized the OTC market as disorganized and fragmented. Recall that OTC stocks are stocks that are traded among brokers, individuals, and dealers, off an organized exchange (e.g., not traded on the NYSE or the AMEX). The SEC recommended an automated system, and the National Association of Securities Dealers (NASD) was commissioned to implement automation of the OTC market. The system became the *NASD Automated Quotations system,* or *Nasdaq.* It was constructed in the late sixties and began trading in February of 1971.

By 1975, stocks that were traded on the Nasdaq had to meet listing requirements that OTC stocks not listed on the Nasdaq did not have to meet. This differentiated the Nasdaq stocks from other OTC stocks. A further differentiation among Nasdaq stocks occurred in 1982, as the best of the Nasdaq split off and formed the Nasdaq National Market. This market is the large-cap market. The small-cap Nasdaq stocks formed the Nasdaq Small-Cap market. In 1984, the Small Order Execution System was created, abbreviated SOES. This is an electronic order routing system that is designed and intended to execute the purchase and sale orders of small investors. SOES is an integral part of the trading tools of the direct access trader, and we will have much more to say about it later. In 1990, the Nasdaq created the Over-the-Counter Bulletin Board (OTCBB). This electronic bulletin board allowed small investors the opportunity to purchase and sell OTC stocks not on the Nasdaq. All this time, the Nasdaq was growing by leaps and bounds. By 1994, it surpassed the NYSE in annual share volume. In 1998, the Nasdaq and the Amex announced a merger, out of which would be created the Nasdaq-Amex Market Group. Today, the Nasdaq National Market lists over 4400 securities that meet the stringent standards of large-cap companies, and the Nasdaq Small-Cap Market lists over 1800 small-cap companies, with some of the highest-growth firms and record-breaking IPOs in history.

Nasdaq Market Structure

The Nasdaq is a completely different market from the NYSE. The concept of a trade floor is completely foreign to the Nasdaq. It is an electronic environment, completely screen-based. The way to think about it is that traders are all in some Internet chat room, buying and selling stock from each other. There is no physical place where people are trading stocks, such as the corner of Wall Street and Broad Street in New York. Trading on the Nasdaq occurs wherever someone has electronic access to the market. This electronic access comes from basically two sources of market participants. They are *market makers* and *electronic communication networks* (ECNs). Market makers are employees of big firms, which represent various interests that will be discussed below. ECNs are electronic marketplaces, like big Internet bulletin boards, where people announce their bids and offers over interlinked computers all over the world. The reason traders can circumvent brokerage firms and trade for themselves is because they have been given access to ECNs and to real-time data and because ECNs have been accepted into the Nasdaq. The point is that if you have a computer and an account with a dealer/broker, you can trade like a market maker, participate actively on the Nasdaq, and invest at the best prices. Following is a list of ECNs.

INSTINET INCA

URL: *www.instinet.com*
SNAIL MAIL: 875 Third Avenue
               New York, NY 10022
PHONE: 212-310-9500

ISLAND (ISLD)

URL: *www.isld.com*
SNAIL MAIL: 50 Broad Street, 6th Floor
               New York, NY 10004
PHONE: 212-231-5000
E-MAIL: *info@isld.com*

NEXTRADE ECN

URL: *www.invest2000.com*
SNAIL MAIL: 301 S. Missouri Avenue
               Clearwater, FL 33756
PHONE: 727-446-6660
E-MAIL: *pimge@sprintmail.com*

ARCHIPELAGO

URL: *www.tradearca.com*
SNAIL MAIL: 100 South Wacker Drive
               Suite 2012
               Chicago, IL 60606
PHONE: 312-960-1696

Figure 4-1. NexTrade home page. (*Courtesy of NexTrade.*)

MARKETXT, INC.

URL: *www.marketxt.com*

SNAIL MAIL: 100 Broadway
New York, NY 10005

FAX: 212-777-7676

Market Makers

The buying and selling of stock on the Nasdaq does not involve a specialist who acts like some sort of fast-talking auctioneer selling off cattle.

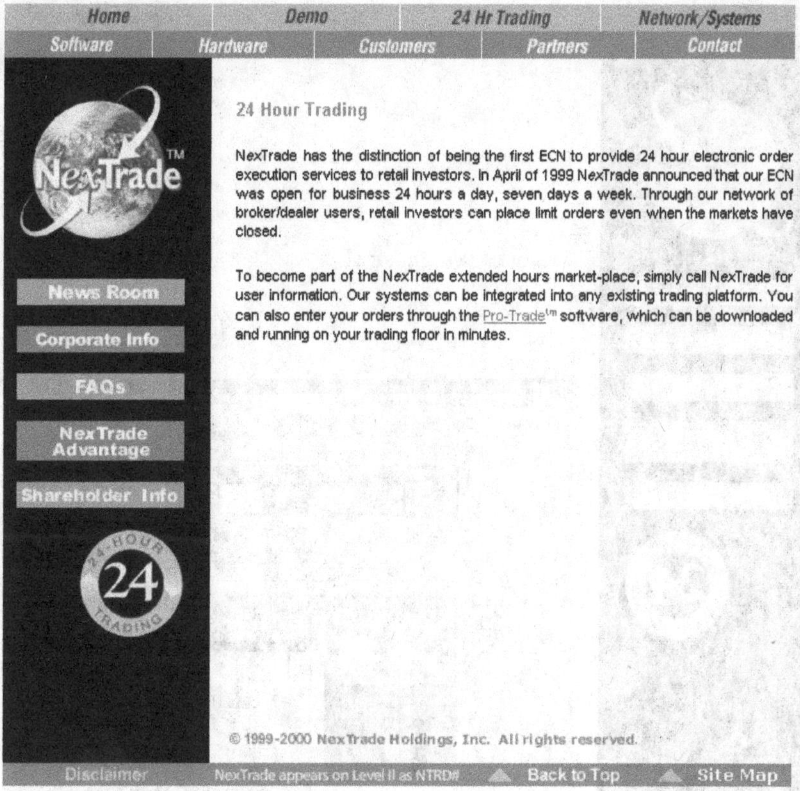

Figure 4-2. NexTrade 24-hour trading. (*Courtesy of NexTrade.*)

That's more the style of the NYSE. The buying and selling of stock on the Nasdaq is similar to a farmer's market, where there are many sellers and buyers. This type of market is called a *dealer-driven market* (you will recall that the NYSE is an auction market). The dealers are the *market makers.* They are agents in the market who are collectively responsible for providing liquidity. They work for big brokerage houses and trade stocks all day for the clients of the brokerage firm. They, as members of the National Association of Securities Dealers, make markets in some of the stocks they trade and are required to maintain a buying and selling presence in these stocks at all times. The role of market maker is a profitable one because of the advantages of the large order flow and inventories of stock, as well as because they make the spreads on their trades.

Each stock on the Nasdaq has multiple market makers who trade in

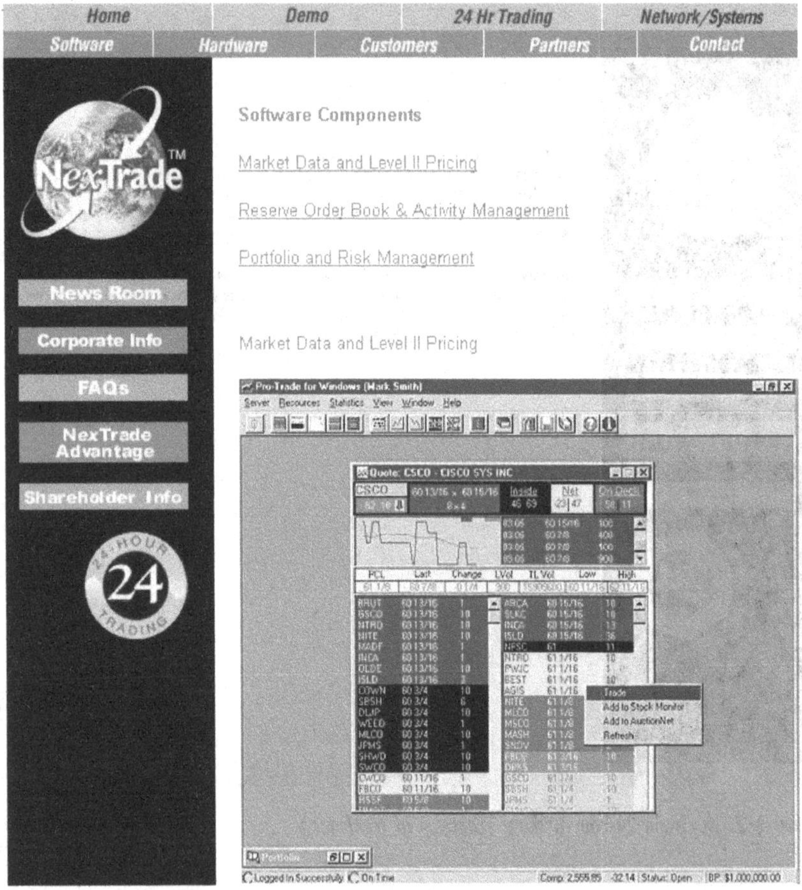

Figure 4-3. NexTrade software components. (*Courtesy of NexTrade.*)

that stock. This is one big difference between the Nasdaq and the NYSE that works in favor of the direct access trader. The groups of market makers as a whole are the ones who must provide this liquidity. If it were just one market maker in charge of maintaining liquidity, the market maker could keep the spreads higher because there would be no competition in the bids and offers. More important, the market maker would know all the order flow for the market. Since there are many market makers, no one market maker has a complete picture of the total stock demanded and the total stock offered. That is, apart from the market order flow known by everyone, the only private information the market maker

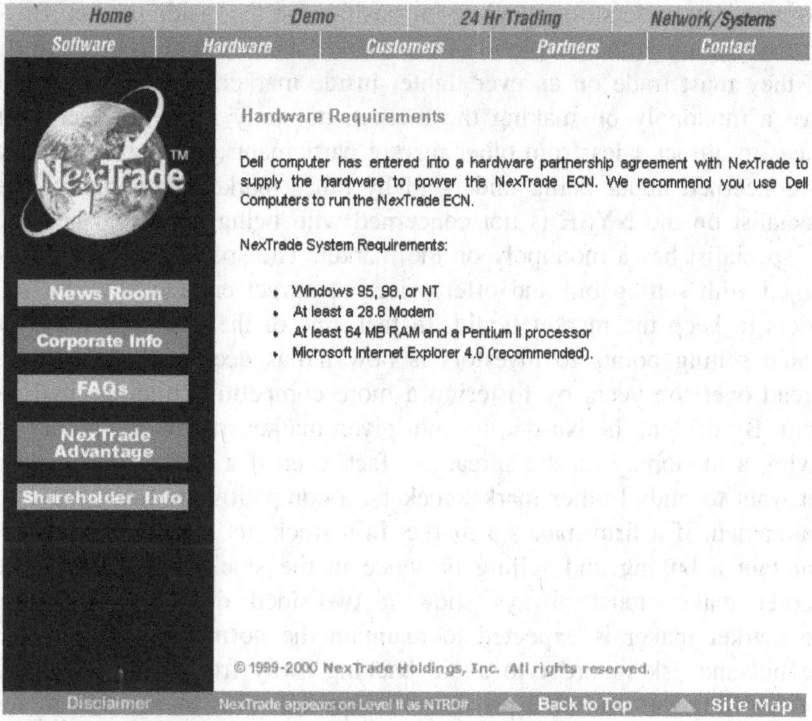

Figure 4-4. NexTrade hardware requirements. (*Courtesy of NexTrade.*)

has is his or her own internal orders. As a result, no one market maker knows for sure where the stock price is going but can only rely on the available market data and knowledge of his or her own order flow. While on the NYSE the specialist knows exactly how much is for sale and how much is demanded of his or her stock, on the Nasdaq, the market makers and the small investors are all in the same boat. In fact, the direct access trader has the same ability to make markets on the Nasdaq that a registered market maker does. The only informational advantage a market maker has on a direct access trader is individual internal order flow. The market maker can only conjecture the aggregate demand and supply for the stock, same as a day trader.

The competition between market makers is also a benefit that works in favor of the Nasdaq direct access trader, but not for the small investor on the NYSE. Because there are many market makers for most stocks, there is a tighter spread between them. As they compete with each other and with day traders, they jockey for position on the inside market. Buying and selling is the lifeblood of the market makers, and in order to do so, they must trade on an ever tighter inside market. Since they do not have a monopoly on making the market, not only must they set their prices to attract sales from other market participants, but they also must be concerned about being undersold by other market participants. The specialist on the NYSE is not concerned with being undersold because the specialist has a monopoly on the market. The specialist is only concerned with setting bid and offer prices to attract enough buy and sell orders to keep the market liquid. In fact, one of the Nasdaq's most repeated selling points to investors is how it has decreased the average spread over the years by fostering a more competitive trading environment. By design, the Nasdaq has not given market makers the luxury of having a monopoly on the spread. In fact, even if a market maker does not want to outbid other market makers, a competitive position must be maintained. If a firm makes a market in a stock, its market maker must maintain a buying and selling presence in the stock at all times. The market maker must always show a two-sided quote. Furthermore, the market maker is expected to maintain the normal spread between the bid and ask in order to avoid backing away from the market and not fulfilling the role of a provider of liquidity. This means that if, for example, the bid is 25 and the ask is $25\frac{1}{8}$, a market maker cannot set the bid price to 23 and the ask price to 29. In doing so, a market maker would not be shouldering the responsibility of providing liquidity, and the other market making firms would not stand for this. Furthermore, market makers are required to comply with the order handling rules of the SEC. These are rules that govern how a buy or sell order should be executed.

It is important to note that the Nasdaq market makers are not competing in such fashion for the benefit of the day trader. The competitiveness of the Nasdaq marketplace, the tight spreads, and so on had to be forced on market makers. They are a result of the lawsuits by small investors and investor groups, litigation and regulation by the SEC, and Justice Department investigations. Nasdaq market makers come to work each morning motivated by the same rational self-interest as the small investor, not altruism. In the past, they have engaged in anticompetitive practices against day traders and small investors in general and have taken advantage of their positions to extract as much of the small investors' money as possible. The entry of day traders and small investors has

threatened the livelihood of those who made their living off these traditional (and high rent) investment channels. Market makers naturally have
opposed this type of change and have had to be forced to adapt to this
new, more competitive marketplace. One example of this is order handling
rules.

   After a Justice Department probe into anticompetitive practices, the
SEC implemented new trading rules in 1997 on the Nasdaq. These rules
governed the handling of orders by market makers. Nowadays, the Nasdaq
Stock Market, Inc., is proud to announce that after they implemented the
order handling rules and began quoting at $\frac{1}{16}$ of a dollar, spreads fell by
40 percent. This begs the question as to what was so revolutionary about
order handling rules that would have this effect and why the Nasdaq had
not implemented this solution sooner. The remarkable change that the
order handling rules brought to the Nasdaq was to implement the same
honest business practices that other marketplaces uphold. These rules simply require market makers to display the best price at which a given issue
is available. That's all. Incredible as it sounds, this simple change reduced
spreads because before implementation of the rule, market makers would,
for example, sell at prices higher than the buy orders they had. They
might not have displayed lower bids or limit orders, or they might have
even reported trades after market hours to prevent traders from acting on
higher prices. For example, if you wanted to sell a stock and the market
maker had a buy order higher than the current bid, the market maker
would buy your stock on the bid and sell it to the other party at their
higher price. Thus, if the market was $138\frac{1}{4} \times 138\frac{1}{2}$ and you placed a
market order to sell, you might get $138\frac{1}{4}$ on the bid. Meanwhile, the
market maker was sitting on an order to buy at $138\frac{3}{8}$ the whole time.
The market maker would sell your stock to that party and pocket the $\frac{1}{8}$
difference. In this example, the market maker was sitting on a bid that
was on the inside of the market but did not give you that price. Order
handling rules prevent this because they force the market maker to display
the best available stock price.

Electronic Communication Networks (ECNs)
ECNs are electronic marketplaces where investors of all sizes can buy
and sell Nasdaq stocks. There are a number of them, and the basic idea
behind them is to provide the electronic interface through which Nasdaq
stocks are traded. Using a terminal or home computer, the electronic
trader sends the order to the trader's order-entry firm. The firm routes the

order to an ECN. The ECN shows the trader's order on its market for the relevant stock, and it appears on the trading screens of other traders and market makers. If other traders or market makers are interested in filling the order, they can do so. On ECNs, electronic direct access traders can place a bid or an offer between the spreads and make the spread on an order. Also, one can trade directly with other traders or market makers on that system.

There are many features relevant to ECNs that the direct access trader should be aware of. Once the investor sends an order in, it becomes part of the market, but there is no guarantee that someone will take the opposite position. This means that your order may not be filled if no one is interested in buying or selling at the price that you specified. In fact, market makers are not required to provide liquidity on ECNs at all. They are noninterventionist markets, and if no one wants to fill your order, you must adjust your price to attract buyers or sellers. However, for this same reason, you can sell at better prices than the market quote if you anticipate investor sentiment and sell ahead of the market. All the buy and sell orders are aggregated on an ECN and appear as one big market demand and supply for the stock at the market price. This aggregation allows market makers anonymity, which is convenient for when they have large blocks of stock to sell but do not want the other market participants to know this. For example, a market maker who has to sell off a large block of stock may repeatedly sell off smaller parcels so as not to cause the offer to fall quickly. On an ECN, no one knows that the market maker is repeatedly selling off stock. However, this aggregation of the stock is also beneficial because it quickly summarizes the demand for, and supply of, the stock on the market. Additionally, there is no limit to the size of an order on an ECN, whereas on SOES there are (see below for SOES). Most ECNs allow stop and limit orders outside the inside market, which is good for exiting trades as planned, instead of trying to escape a market that is moving against you. Finally, in the case that the market is moving against you, the ECNs will not partially fill your order as you try to exit your position.

There are a number of ECNs. Many offer after-hours trading, and they differ in the fee structure, volume, and traders they attract. Table 4-1 lists some of the most popular ECNs and the symbol they will appear under on your trade screen.

Each ECN varies in trading fees, clientele, and trade volume. Instinet Corp., which is owned by Reuters, and The Island, which is owned by

TABLE 4–1. POPULAR ECNs	
Archipelago LLC	ARCA
Attain	ATTN
Bloomberg Trade LLC	BTRD
Brass Securities	BRUT
Instinet Corp.	INCA
The Island	ISLD
NexTrade	NTRD
Spear Leeds	REDI
Strike Technologies	STRK

Datek Corp., are the first and second in terms of volume. Volume, as we will see later, is a key element in ensuring liquidity. Archipelago LLC and The Island are lower-cost ECNs. Finally, in terms of clientele, Instinet Corp. has the most professional trading market of all the ECNs except one, which deserves special mention, called SelectNet.

SelectNet

SelectNet is the ECN of the Nasdaq market makers. It is their internal trading system. A day trader who places an order through SelectNet may either *preference* or *broadcast* the order. To preference the order means that you select a specific market maker and send that market maker the order. To broadcast the order means that you display the order to all the market makers. Market makers on SelectNet are not obligated to fulfill orders, however. If you preference them, it is because you are buying or selling on their terms. Note, however, that you will be trading with market makers only. No day traders will see your order if you broadcast it on SelectNet. Only market makers see orders on SelectNet; they do not show up on the screens of day traders. This implies that if you trade through SelectNet, on the opposite end of the trade are some of the most astute traders on Wall Street. It is possible to outmaneuver them occasionally, but it is not wise to underestimate them or to make it policy to trade against them. These are professionals who trade for a living every work-day and have a lot on the ball.

Another important point: SelectNet does not allow limit or stop orders for limit or trigger prices not between the spread. That is, you cannot place a limit order if the limit price is not between the bid price and the ask price. If, for example, you see that Intel is

$$\text{INTC} \qquad 86\tfrac{1}{8} \times 86\tfrac{3}{8} \qquad 1000 \times 1000$$

and you are long on the stock, you may wish to set a buy limit order at 86 to cover a potential fall in the price. However, SelectNet will not allow you to do this. Limit orders are an important tool for the day trader, and the inability to fully utilize them on SelectNet makes it less attractive than other ECNs.

Small Order Execution System (SOES)

SOES is another type of electronic network linking market makers to direct access traders and individual investors. This system was created in 1984 to free up market makers' time. Its intent was to allow the small investor access to the markets in a more efficient manner. However, market makers abused the system consistently, and finally, in the stock market crash of October of 1987, the problem came to a head.

For years, market makers had filled orders at prices that benefited them when investors placed market orders and the stock prices were moving around. For example, an investor may have placed a buy market order thinking to get the market price of 25, but if the stock were moving up, the market maker might sell the stock at the price $25\tfrac{1}{8}$. This $\tfrac{1}{8}$ of a point represents $125 lost to the small investor on a 1000-share block. This is money that the market makers would extract from the small investors all the time. Finally, during the stock market crash, as small investors tried frantically to get out of the market, most brokers did not answer their phones and did not tend to their investors. Even if they had, most market makers refused to participate in SOES or to provide liquidity to such a tumbling market.

SOES at that point had not been a mandatory system for market makers to participate in. After the crash, however, it was widely perceived that the large institutional traders on the market had unfairly had more market access due to their clout. That is, mutual funds and pension funds were able to liquidate their positions during the crash because they are big investment interests, whereas small investors had to take the loss. As a result, the NASD made participation in the SOES mandatory for all registered market makers.

SOES was reorganized in the following manner: A 1000-share maximum order size was maintained for SOES. A market maker participating in the market for a given stock was responsible for filling orders up to twice the maximum order size, i.e., 2000 shares, if

1   The market maker's ask or bid price was the market ask or bid price.
2   If individual investors preferenced him or her.

Furthermore, the 1000-share limit was to be in effect for any continuous 5-minute period. This means that one cannot sell 1000 shares and 3 seconds later sell 1000 shares again using SOES. Furthermore, one cannot use different accounts to sell many blocks of 1000 shares when all the accounts belong to the same individual. Finally, the usual short-sale rules of not selling on a down or zero minus bid apply.

SOES is the safety net of the individual investor and the direct access trader. When day trading, it is safer to buy and sell blocks of shares no bigger than 1000 shares. SOES can then be used to quickly get out of a bad trade or when the market turns against you. With SOES, a market maker must buy or sell you 1000 shares at the market quote corresponding to the time you place the buy or sell order. Market makers can no longer sell you shares at higher prices or buy your shares at lower prices because the price moved between the time you ordered and the time they fill the order. This change has led the market makers to create the terms "SOES bandit" and "getting SOESed." They refer to a small investor who is simply exercising the right to buy or sell stock at the price going on the market when placing the buy or sell order. It is ironic that the people buying or selling at the market price are called bandits and not the market makers who want to sell at a different price. One would think it would be the other way around.

What is important to remember is that SOES can only be used once every 5 minutes and only to buy or sell a maximum of 1000 shares. Also, the usual short-sale rules apply, i.e., no selling on a down bid. Observing these rules gives the direct access trader a safety net allowing access to liquidity within a reasonable time frame. This helps to lower the risks of trading.

Accessing the Nasdaq market stocks for the position trader is the same as accessing the NYSE stocks. Whether employing a broker or some broker/dealer service for online trading, both give access to markets within reasonable time periods for the purposes of position trading. The position trader may look at the current size and price of the market and the stock's performance over time, analyst reports, press releases, and other things. For this reason, the position trader does not need to know the exact price of the stock every instant that passes. The position trader is more interested in the price of a stock within a neighborhood of a day and how that price may change over the investment horizon. The timing of the trade for a position trader is calculated in weeks or months. Such traders may look at 3-month, 6-month, or 1-year charts. If this is the case, then the position trader may not be distraught if the stock price moves up $13/16$ of a point. If the position trader buys 100 shares, however, this small move cost him $81.25. For this reason alone, direct access benefits the position trader.

A trader investing for a shorter horizon must look at the price movement of a stock for the last 5 minutes or maybe even less. The trader is interested in how the stock price is moving in a very short time span. In some cases, day traders may buy blocks of stock of up to 1000 shares; some traders buy even more. For the same price movement that the position trader faced, $13/16$ of a point, the day trader loses $812. That is, $13/16$ of a dollar is lost on each share, and there are 1000 shares, so the loss amounts to $13/16 \times 1000$, which is $812. Obviously, a trading method where such losses are common becomes unsustainable. For this reason, direct access traders must access real-time data and have the clearest picture of the current market available. They use instantaneous execution of trades because a few seconds can mean the difference between being in the money or out of the money. We will say more about the technology that makes day trading possible in the coming chapters. For now, what is important is that the Nasdaq markets make enough information available for the day trader to get a clear picture of the market.

This information is necessary because market news gets old really fast for direct access traders. For this reason, the Nasdaq provides its data in real time to subscribers. Real-time data means that you see what is happening as it happens; no one sees it before you do. Delayed market quotes are of little use. For day trading, you need nothing less than real-time quotes. The new electronic environment available to the small investor provides the real-time data in three levels. They are appropriately called *level I, level II,* and *level III.*

Level I data are the basic market quotes. That is, a level I real-time quote includes the current market bid and ask, as well as the size of the market. This is not enough of a picture of the market for active trading, but it can suffice for position trading.

Level II data are given on the workhorse data screen. Most electronic direct access traders have trading screens with level II data. This screen includes the current market bid and ask for a number of stocks that are chosen by the trader, just like level I. Level II, however, also includes the market makers interested in bidding or offering the stocks of interest.

Also included are the prices at which each market maker is bidding or offering. Furthermore, there are minute-by-minute charts on price and volume changes available to help the day trader discern where the momentum is swinging. There are charts for market indicators and many other options. This technology is the tool that makes day trading accessible and trading more profitable for all kinds of traders, be they day traders or otherwise.

Level III data are given on a data screen for market makers where they can refresh their bids. It offers the same data information as level II; the only difference is that market makers use level III because it gives them the clearance to update their bids. These three types of data are the pictures of the market available to investors. They are the best description available for discerning where the market may move. These data are one of the key tools for electronic direct access traders; as it becomes more widely available and less expensive, more small investors are making the jump from online or other types of investing to direct access trading.

This chapter has shown the basic market environment in which traders conduct business on a daily basis. We concentrated on the New York Stock Exchange and the Nasdaq markets and outlined the basic differences and similarities of trading on each. We looked at the types of orders that are available to investors and the different restrictions that investors can use to control and manage their risk. Having seen how the markets work as a medium for trading, in the next chapter we will look at the new trading opportunities that electronic direct access trading offers. We will look at what this type of trading means and what opportunities it offers to the small investor.

QUESTIONS

1   What sort of restrictions on orders or what types of orders are most useful for guarding against losses?

2   When does the use of limit orders and stop orders become so mechanical and restrictive that the investor is limiting his or her own earning potential by using them?

3   Are IPOs in any way an investment opportunity for the small investor? Why or why not?

4   When do the advantages of a dealer-driven market turn against the small investor?

5   Which ECNs have the most small investor friendly trading environment?

5

TRADING WITH DIRECT ACCESS

So far we have looked at the basics of investing in the markets. In Chapter 2 we saw some of the different avenues available for investing, such as brokers and mutual funds. Each of these investment avenues implies costs that in the end are paid for by investors. It is only logical that these investors know why they shoulder the burden of these costs and where they are derived from. For many small investors, electronic direct access trading offers many advantages relative to these other avenues. For small investors now investing online, for example, there are many potential advantages to this new investment medium, and it behooves them to know where these advantages come from. As we shall see, electronic direct access trading offers better prices, more information, and better investing opportunities. For those who are able to exploit these new opportunities, a better avenue for their investment dollars lies in the ability to electronically access the markets described in

Chapter 3. These markets are the means by which investors come to-
gether. They are where the opportunities lie, and electronic direct access
can give the small investor a way into these markets that never existed
before. This chapter will take a closer look at how the small investor
can capitalize on these opportunities.

Many who invest through a traditional broker, an online investment
firm, or otherwise are skeptical of whether there really is a new, more
powerful way to invest. I have referred throughout this book to the new
means of investing—it is electronic direct access trading. Much the same
way that the automobile revolutionized the landscapes of cities and lifestyles of Americans, the new trading technology that has emerged will
change the landscape of investing and certainly the lifestyles of those able
to adapt and capitalize on it. The automobile was referred to as the "rich
man's toy," but it has integrated itself into the core of everyday life and
proven to be a technology with staying power. In much the same way,
the technology that has made electronic direct access possible is sometimes described as marginal, for day traders and fringe investors. This
technology, however, is poised to grow and replace the inefficient investment vehicles currently used because it saves people money. It has spun
off from day trading technology and commercially available Internet technology in general. Day traders actively use direct access technology and
have pushed its development in recent years, and the Internet is bringing
these tools to all small investors. This chapter focuses closely on what
this medium of investing is exactly and how it generates new and profitable investment opportunities for investors, large or small.

As we shall see, with the growth of this new technology, the markets
have never been more able to absorb new investors. The ability to make
the jump into direct access trading is the key to taking advantage of the
newly created opportunities. The markets are wide open for those wishing
to end their reliance on the old ways of investing. By making the transition into more advanced trading systems, investors looking to participate
in the markets will no longer be subject to the high commissions from
which Wall Street companies have made their living for years. This technology was invented precisely to circumvent the stranglehold that Wall
Street had on the markets and provide direct access to small investors.
Electronic direct access represents the ability for the small investor to
participate in the markets without having to stuff the pockets of the Wall
Street big shots along the way. With it, investors can concentrate on the

business of finding a good investment, and they can take risks for their own sake and not bear a big risk only to see half their reward taken by their brokerage firm.

Brokerage firms are quickly realizing that the competition from direct access technology provides individuals with an alternative where they do not lose money to commissions and slippage. Recall how trading through brokers generates these losses for the small investor. Suppose, for example, three individuals, call them Al, Linda, and Carl, invest in some stock, call it XYZ. Suppose that Al sells 200 shares of XYZ short, and Linda and Carl each buy 100 shares of XYZ. Now, the price of XYZ falls from 100 to 97. Al buys back the 200 shares he sold short and makes $600 profit (and this would be an extremely good trade, given that the price moved 3 points). But this is not really Al's total profit because he has to pay commissions on the short sale and the buyback, and he most likely lost money to slippage because the markets moved too quickly for him to buy at 97 or sell at 100. Suppose that these losses amount to only $50. Linda and Carl both lost $300, but they also lost to commissions and slippage, say, about $50 each. Looking at the big picture, Linda and Carl suffered a $700 loss, whereas Al earned a $550 profit, so the brokers kept $150 from the whole deal. These three investors essentially took opposite sides of a $600 bet, and the brokers ended up taking $150 from them, risk-free. This is 25 percent of the earnings, risk-free. It is easy to see why investors are turning to other methods of investing.

The term *electronic direct access trading* (EDAT) refers to the way technology has been combined to give individuals not affiliated with brokerage firms access to markets as if they had a seat on an exchange. Incredibly, electronic direct access simply makes buying and selling on the stock markets much like buying and selling anywhere else. Technically, what electronic direct access does is combine the availability of real-time information about the performance of the Nasdaq with the ability to trade like a market maker. Dealings occur directly with other investors or market makers on the different electronic trading venues. Having real-time information means that as an investor you can know exactly what is going on in the markets as it happens. With EDAT, the prices you see are the prices of the stocks at that instant, not the price of the stock 15 minutes ago. Recall that the markets are very volatile at times so that stock prices from 30 seconds ago are yesterday's news for investors.

Having the ability to trade directly like a market maker means that you have the ability to act on your information directly and not through a third party. You can buy or sell your stock electronically to other traders or market makers and not have to ask a brokerage firm to buy or sell for you. To better understand what EDAT means to stock markets, imagine that stocks were like cars, but again, no one cares if the car is used. If you wanted to buy or sell a car, you could ask a dealer how much the car is worth. The dealer would give you a price and then turn around and sell the car to someone else. This would be akin to asking a big brokerage firm to sell your stock. Trading with EDAT would allow you to read the automobile section of the classifieds, see how much cars are going for, and place an ad so as to sell your car directly to an interested buyer. In this way, you are able to sell at a higher price, and the buyer can buy at a lower price, because you have eliminated the dealer from the process.

In years past, only a major brokerage firm could keep a constant watch on the movements of the stock markets. This is no longer the case, however, due to the progress of technology. The combination of the affordability of personal computers and the proliferation of Internet software has made this monopoly of real-time information on stock markets a thing of the past. The wealth of information available to the small investor and the low cost of acquiring it have generated great interest in the stock markets. In fact, it is online investing that has benefited the most from the proliferation of stock market information. Investors have fueled online firms' growth for years, as individuals have sought a better way to invest. Along with the push for lower connectivity costs, better access to information about the markets, and better research, investors have pushed for fairer, more equitable access to the markets. These efforts have resulted in the development of real-time information technology for markets and the ability to gain access to the markets without having to go through the large brokerage firms.

An investor today can take advantage of electronic direct access trading to invest in Nasdaq stocks. Recall that the Nasdaq is the electronic market; hence it is the market where EDAT traders operate. The secret to trading with direct electronic access is the ability to trade on *electronic communication networks* (ECNs). They are the heart of the new trading environment in which Wall Street's most powerful trade alongside any investor with a computer and a modem. This is the beauty of an ECN. Whereas a few years ago, to trade a stock, you would have had to essentially pay a firm to trade for you, now you can do it yourself. As opposed to trading through an online brokerage firm, where essentially you are emailing some broker an order, on an ECN you buy from or sell to another market participant directly. The simple ability to buy and sell from whom you chose directly, rather than through a third party, is a large part of the revolutionary change that has dramatically transformed how business is done on Wall Street.

The other part of the revolutionary change transforming the markets is the information component to direct access. Trading on an ECN requires having information about trade volume and price movement. This information is essential for the investment decision. This real-time information is available to EDAT investors so that they can trade with their eyes open and get as clear a picture of the markets as the other market participants, such as brokerage firms. Investors with Nasdaq level II data are the ones who have the essential information for trading. They know the most up-to-date quotes, the interest in the stock, and whether market participants are lining up to buy or sell. This is an indispensable part of any EDAT trader's tools. Using level II data, a direct access trader can get as clear a picture of market demand and supply as is available to the large Wall Street firms. This type of information serves as the eyes and ears of a trader in the market. Since the Nasdaq is so fragmented, this information is the only way to have some idea of what traders as a group are thinking. Without this information, trying to gauge the market is impossible because there are as many individual decisions taking place as computers connected to the Nasdaq.

If we think in terms of the car market example, trading without this information and instead using delayed quotes is like trying to sell your car based on last year's prices. The dealer with the current information obviously has an advantage. With the availability of Nasdaq level II data, however, you no longer trade at a disadvantage. You can trade with the confidence of knowing the exact prices and quantities on the market and not lose money to big firms because they had better information about what was going on at the time of your trade.

This technology is changing the way business gets done in the equity markets and redistributing the profits of stock trading away from big firms and toward those who can read the market accurately. It is no longer true that the employees of large brokerage firms and a few select traders are the only ones who can make a living trading stocks. Direct access technology has circumvented the barriers to equities markets. The elite Wall

Street firms now must earn their profits by trading rather than by exploiting their monopoly on market access through astronomical commissions, slippage, and payment for order flow.

Apart from the obvious advantages of better prices and more information for trading equity, this technology draws in all sorts of investors because it offers the flexibility and individuality that appeals to individuals from all walks of life. Many employees of Wall Street brokerage houses have left their positions to exploit their market knowledge for their own personal gain rather than for the benefit of their firms. In addition to keeping more of the gains from the risks they take, these individuals enjoy more flexibility in making their own schedules and organizing their work routine without having to deal with the constraints of a large, rigid corporate structure. However, having intimate knowledge of the markets is not a prerequisite to using direct access trading. People from many careers and backgrounds have traded successfully with this technology. Some are drawn to direct access because of its entrepreneurial environment. The structure of the markets with direct access is such that one can enter and work as a small investor, and in fact, many people do this for a living. Many online investors participate in direct access trading because of its superiority over their online brokers. They abandon the delayed and sluggish trading and the costs that result because of the inefficiency of online brokers. Remember that online brokers are just a fancy way to email an order to a large Wall Street firm. It is ironic that the same appeal that drew investors away from retail stockbrokers to online investing is now drawing investors away from online brokers to electronic direct access trading. This appeal is based on better prices, more information, and a better investment return for investors.

These individuals are all drawn to direct access trading because they realize that as long as they are taking risks in investing, they should capture as much of the reward realized from the investment as possible. By providing the trader with the best information, the trader gets the best possible picture of the market available. Through better information, direct access helps reduce the risk an investor takes. Direct access offers the clearest and most current picture of the market available. With this information, the direct access trader can concentrate on interpreting market conditions and focus on prospective trades. No longer must investors guess as to how the markets are doing and find out too late that they guessed wrong. The direct access traders have as much information as is publicly available to any other market participant. They can use this information to try to project the future path of stock prices rather than imagine where the current market position may be. Leading indicators such as volume, the market indices, and daily charts are all essential for getting a clear picture of the market. Without these, the trader is guessing more than necessary and, as a result, taking a bigger financial risk. Additionally, direct access allows the investor to keep as much of the return on the investment as possible by eliminating the Wall Street intermediaries. Direct access charges eliminate slippage, offering the opportunity to trade at the best prices available.

Naturally, Wall Street is not standing idly by watching the surge in electronic trading. Brokers and large Wall Street firms have fought the amplification of electronic trading at every step of its development. The Securities and Exchange Commission (SEC) has had to force Short Order Execution System (SOES) participation so that market makers fulfill their roles as providers of liquidity. Additionally, Wall Street firms have attempted to disparage day traders in the media, as well as present themselves as the protectors of the small investor and the savvy market investors who put their expertise to work for you. However, as we saw in Chapter 4, they have no real incentive to do this. In fact, the same Wall Street firms that have attempted to abolish day traders are the ones who are aggressively investing in the companies that run the systems and develop the technology for day trading.

Wall Street is now actively seeking the same firms that spawned the day trading technology and were vilified by Wall Street as "SOES bandits." These firms are pushing the development of ECNs and their expansion. The day trading community has pushed to open up markets and to deregulate investment opportunities so as to allow small investors to participate individually. Now this technology is growing beyond just day traders and is available to anyone interested in investing electronically. Currently, ECNs handle over 30 percent of the trades on the Nasdaq and are projected to handle over 50 percent by early 2001. Large Wall Street firms such as Merrill Lynch, Goldman Sachs, Lehman Brothers, and many others have realized that the future of trading lies in electronic direct access. The point is that these firms have supported the technology of direct access with their wallets, if not with their rhetoric. They have scrambled to buy into ECNs as they realized that the order routing technology of day traders is quickly spreading to all kinds of investors. After years of ignoring the technology of direct electronic access to markets, the Wall Street firms are now in the precarious position of having to play catch-up in the markets rather than setting the trends. Imagine what it must have been like for many of the most renowned firms on Wall Street to find themselves years behind in the technology of financial markets. In response, many of these firms have bought into three or four ECNs. They have no idea as to which ECN will carry the most trade volume and thus are hedging in their attempt to play some role in the expansion of virtual markets.

As investors are trading among themselves on ECNs, the big market makers now represent simply one more group of participants in the fray of daily trading. The success of these trading venues, however, depends on the volume of participation. As more people log on to and trade using an ECN, there will be more purchases and sales of stocks, which will make that ECN a better market for trading. In order for an ECN to be successful, there needs to be enough people buying and selling so that orders can be filled easily on it. This is an important principle to know and one that traders always keep an eye on. Volume in a market is the key to liquidity. The more liquid a market is, the more it will attract liquidity. This is interesting to note because as the virtual markets have grown in past years, this growth only makes them more attractive and more effective places to trade. The more they grow, the better and more quickly they can fill orders. This virtuous cycle drives their growth, in that the more they grow, the better they are for trading, and thus the more they will grow.

The need for trading volume on an ECN is a phenomenon that has led many to predict that they will consolidate into a few major ECNs. In this way there would be just a few electronic meeting places for buyers and sellers of Nasdaq stocks rather than many small electronic markets, where you may have trouble finding the best price. In fact, some have gone so far as to criticize ECNs for fragmenting liquidity in markets and making it more difficult for buyers and sellers to find the best prices for their orders. That is, some have argued that having many ECNs is bad because it makes it more difficult to find the best prices and buyers. Similarly, one could argue that having too many stores in a shopping mall can make it time-consuming to search for the best bargain among all of them.

In response to the potential problem of fragmented liquidity on ECNs, an interesting solution has been the emergence of "smart" systems. These are electronic portals for traders that search out the best possible price among all the ECNs. They operate like a search engine that rather than looking to see if your order can be filled on one ECN or another, looks for the best possible place to fill your order among all the ECNs. Thus, using our example, a smart system would be like a person who knows all the prices of the stores at the mall and can tell you immediately where the best bargain is. Suppose that you wanted to buy 100 shares of ABC stock. A direct access trader could look to see how much the ask price is on some ECNs, maybe Archipelago and The Island. The same trader could go to one of these trading portals, place an order, and the system would search among all the registered ECNs to see which has the best price. In this sense, these smart systems are the next generation of trading technology in that they further work to match up the trader's order with the best possible price.

Wall Street has noticed this next generation of trading technology and has attempted to position itself with companies such as TradeScape.com, whose system searches through all the available ECNs to find the best price for the trader. The Wall Street firms have realized that the technology gap between the best online broker and the direct access technology of an ECN portal is too large to bridge on their own. Tradescape, for example, advertises that its portal can search through all the existing ECNs within 17 milliseconds (ms) for the best price on an order. Imagine trading in the opening of the trading day with this kind of technology at your fingertips. In the frenzy of the market openings, you would never want to use an online broker or, much less, telephone a broker again. Wall Street firms have already begun to align themselves with this type of technology because they are years behind in its development.

This type of technology benefits the trader in that it works toward making the individual's job consist solely of deciding which is the best stock to buy. When trading, it is of fundamental importance to stick to the issue at hand, which is anticipating market sentiment and taking positions with split-second precision. Having to search across ECNs while concentrating on the movement of a stock price only adds to the workload of the trader.

In fact, direct access accounts allow individuals to set up their trading screens in the way that is most convenient and comfortable for them to trade. In the language of computer programmers, the programs that run these screens are called *user-interface protocols* (UIPs). The sole purpose of these UIPs is to make life as easy as possible for the trader. The trading screens are set up like a Windows environment, where you can see charts, lists of stocks, and prices that you are interested in following. These screens are designed to make the process of trading user-friendly and transmission of information more effective for the trader. The complicated algorithms on which they are based are functioning in the background, while the user is unaware of them and can concentrate on picking the right stocks. The next-generation portals attempt to go a step further by eliminating the time and effort of searching for the best possible price for an order. In a fraction of a second, these portals search out and fill the order of the direct access trader. They are a very promising tool for EDAT trading and are poised to grow tremendously as electronic markets continue to develop.

Already markets are showing an influx of traders as new investors join in for the first time or make the jump from online investing or brokered trading. Many individuals are drawn to the unique freedom that direct access traders enjoy. Some are day trading and scalping profits from intraday price movements on stocks. Others are swing trading and capturing movements in stock price trends over a few days or weeks, whereas still others are in for the long term. Direct access allows these investors to make their own schedules and trade as they please. Be aware, however, that direct access trading is not an investment activity that is to be taken lightly. Depending on the method of trading, it can require 100 percent concentration and certainly a commitment to learning by all kinds of investors. The markets are a place where everyone is looking to make money. Keep in mind, however, that because you are buying and selling from other traders, if you are making money, it is because others are losing it. Although no one enters with the intention of losing money, many people will. The ones losing money may be mentally unprepared for the dynamics of the markets and the fast-paced changes that occur. However good the strategy of a trader, avoiding consistent losses is not about strategies or luck—it is about sticking to basic market survival skills.

Discipline, learning, and intuition are the best tools of any trader, and this is especially true of the direct access trader. Because of the power of direct access trading, it is especially important to conduct oneself with discipline, learning, and intuition. Mistakes can lead to big losses because of the power of direct access trading. It is a powerful tool, and much the same way that one would not play around with a dangerous weapon, one should not wager one's money carelessly with a direct access trading.

The discipline involves starting out with a reasonable trading strategy and sticking with it. Sometimes, amid all the ballyhooing about technological advances and complex financial market structures, we forget the simple lessons that get us through everyday life. The simple fact is that direct access trading is a medium for investing and making money. Traders look at it as just a useful tool for a job or a way of earning a living. Those who have the discipline to divorce their emotions from the decision-making process of buying or selling are the most successful. Trading one's own money can be a nerve-racking experience, and the thrill of making a successful trade and working among the exciting opportunities is a large part of the appeal for some traders. The successful ones, however, try to keep their emotions as far from influencing their assessments of the markets as possible. Let your emotions motivate you to work harder to protect your money and watch it grow. Your emotions can be constructive if they push you to study the markets harder and learn more about trading strategies. Do not let your emotions guide your investment choices. It is better to make a good choice than to try to get lucky with your stock picks. If you are betting on sheer luck or hoping for a miracle, you have come to the wrong place. Serious traders do not gamble with savings on the markets any more than they would gamble with savings in Las Vegas and call that investing. And yet, while no one would ever admit to this, many investors ignore the warning signs of their own trading systems. They do not exercise the discipline required to trade based on their strategy rather than based on luck.

This is important for every trader making the jump from online investing to direct access trading. With direct access, trading becomes much more dynamic and much more exciting. The adrenaline rush from the power of this technology can lead to costly mistakes for the undisciplined direct access trader. Some stocks can change momentum in seconds or minutes. The precious moments to get in or out of trades are not to be lost to wallowing or self-gratifying contemplation. Instead of concentrating on how great or bad things are, concentrate on making money, which is what trading is about. Having the discipline to stay focused on the trading is what allows individuals to fully exploit the speed of direct access trading during the brief moments when opportunities arise. This is especially true for bad trades, although it is also true for good ones. People recoil quickly in the face of losses; in fact, economists and financial analysts have strong evidence of this behavior in markets and model them accordingly. However, it is being able to control losses, which are inevitable, that will keep traders in the game for the long haul. Trading without controlling losses is like driving without looking at how much gas is left in the tank. No one would attempt to drive anywhere without making sure they had enough gas available. Similarly, no successful trading strategy will function without making sure that losses are kept to a minimum and the stock of money available for investment is kept under control. The difficulty is not in devising such an investment plan but rather in not deviating from it. And one must have the discipline not to act compulsively or let hope and fears govern trading.

Having discipline will force you, throughout your trading, to stick to your strategy. The strategies are as different as the traders themselves, which is to be expected because they are all meant to fulfill the individual trader's investment goals. Some traders use direct access to the markets for trading at the best prices, even though they are investing for the long run. They use direct access to save on commissions, to minimize slippage, and to efficiently exit a bad position. Others use direct access to trade with short-run momentum. These individuals may keep a trade for a few days or a week. A third group may use direct access to trade mainly intraday but keep some positions overnight or even for a day or two. Finally, some people are pure day traders, scalping profits from short-term movements in stocks and closing out their positions at the end of each day. When making the jump from another trading medium, such as online investing, to direct access trading, your strategy for employing the new investment tools will depend on which group you wish to belong to. Once having decided your investment goals, it will be mental discipline that will decide if you attain your goals or not.

In trading, impulsive bets have no place. Those who trade this way will lose money because they do not come to work, they come to entertain themselves with the stock market. There is no room for entertainment in a successful trading strategy. The closeness to the markets, the sharp gains, and the risk may appeal to people attracted to gaming, but this will lead to heavy losses. The Nasdaq is not a casino. The markets are not a place to bear unnecessary risk for the sake of thrill seeking. An individual looking for an adrenaline rush should go skydiving and turn to trading only with both feet firmly planted on the ground and an interest in making money. Traders often boast about the level of risk they handle, and the thrill of the markets has even been glamorized in some big movies. What is important to remember is that often people boasting about the risk they have endured successfully may be exaggerating. What is more, they may "forget" to tell you about the other dozen times they took losses because of the same kind of risk. The question then becomes whether the adrenaline rush from the markets is worth it in the face of these kinds of losses. Furthermore, it is hardly worth mentioning that the risk-taking Wall Street hot shots portrayed by Hollywood are as fake as Peter Pan and Darth Vader. What is real is the amount of money that could be lost in getting caught up in the commotion of investing in the markets. The adrenaline will no doubt affect traders of all types, but successful traders keep their poise and concentrate on the business of making money.

And the times when a trade goes bad are the most difficult to watch. They, however, are inevitable for any kind of investor. This is important to reiterate. It is common to enter into bad trades; the fact that a trade did not turn out to be successful does not signify a mistake or a bad strategy. It is fine, so long as you were in the trade because it made sense and had the discipline to exit when things did not go your way. Watching a stock price fall and hoping that it will recover is the worst thing that you can do. If it does not recover, waiting only adds to your losses. If it does recover, you will have reinforced undisciplined behavior. Saving that one trade will lead to more departures from your trading strategy, impulsive decision making, ad hoc judgments, and certain failure. The successful trader realizes that the power of direct access lies in being able to exit a bad trade quickly, much more quickly than with online trading or trading through the broker. What is the sense of having all the information on markets' demand and the ability to get out with split-second order execution if you just sit on a bad trade and watch it get worse? With direct access, the trader can move on to a profitable trade, having limited the losses on the bad trade, rather than sit and hope that it rebounds in the long run. In order to do so, the trader must have the discipline to absorb small losses as a part of the strategy designed to attain investment goals.

Furthermore, remember whom you are up against in the markets. Professional traders in big Wall Street firms are not gambling away their own money; they are investing their firms' money. They have more to invest and usually a lot of experience on their side. More important, they have no emotional ties to the money that they invest. Because it is not their hard-earned savings, they will not waste time exiting a bad trade. They have strict rules about their maximum exposure and their maximum losses, and they have no problem sticking to them. This is part of the reason why they are successful. If you are to succeed, you also must trade to make money, not to feel good. Use your emotions to drive your efforts to improve yourself as a trader and your concentration. In this way you will have turned the tables on the Wall Street professionals, because this is what they are lacking. The fact that the big firms' staff traders have no emotional ties to their losses helps in maintaining discipline in closing out their positions when bad trades occur. But they also have a lot less incentive to succeed with the money they are investing. Since they do not see 100 percent of the gains from their work, they will have less of an incentive to work hard than will the small investor. This is a classic problem for managers of all kinds of large corporate structures. You are the small investor, so you will protect your investment and work harder to see it grow. Do not let this asset turn into a liability by not exiting bad trades in an efficient manner.

Learning is the second tool that a direct access trader uses to fulfill investment goals. As the old adage reminds us, "Humility is a virtue all preach, none practice, and yet everybody is content to hear." Everyone can learn from his or her mistakes and from the work of others. It should be blatantly obvious that no one is exactly sure of the determinants of stock price movement. There is a lot of work yet to be done in discovering these determinants. Astute traders will learn as markets develop and will adapt. There is no room for complacency in these markets, where there is so much money at stake. Every day new technology improves the information available to investors and the possibilities of trading. The astute trader stays current on new developments and keeps abreast of the market sentiment and the trends in thinking. We must all learn about what is going on in the market because the market price is a result of the group outcome. If one trader is working with obsolete trading styles, he or she will lose on his or her trades.

As the market sentiment changes, so will the behavior of the stock price. The direct access trader will learn how to adjust his or her trading strategy and where possible losses lie ahead. Simply paying lip service to keeping up with the markets will not be enough to maintain your money. In this sense, direct access trading is no different than online investing. It is your money that is at risk in the markets, so you must step up to your responsibility and protect your investment by being an informed trader. The advantage is that with direct access, you have a wealth of information available in real time and the ability to exit trades quickly and cheaply. Learning about investing and trading strategies, practicing and watching the markets closely, analyzing mistakes, and learning from others are all simple ways to further add to the probability of success in trading and investing.

The final tool of the direct access trader is intuition and instinct. The reason this point is worth stressing is because like in so many other competitive areas of life, *the only person you can trust to tell you what is truly in your best interest is yourself.* Direct access trading offers all the tools necessary for success and independence. A direct access trader is as free to lose a fortune as to make one. No matter how great or small, the losses of one trader do not affect the returns of another. Traders are free to self-destruct; it is not in the interest of anyone to stop them from their own irresponsibility. Because no one has an incentive to control another trader's irresponsibility, the only warning one receives is one's own intuition. The most important manifestation of how instinct helps a trader is self-preservation. The instinct for self-preservation allows a trader to bear the sole responsibility of managing the account without the need for some kind of safety net. Sometimes traders do not realize that they are ignoring the fact that in the markets one is on one's own. Because of this problem, traders may ignore their intuition after a string of successful trades. Many times pride and arrogance arise as side effects of success. This can silence the prudent intuition of a trader and lead to self-destructive trading. There is a vicious cycle into which a trader can fall. After a rash of good trades, the trader may take on an unnecessarily aggressive and careless trading style because of unrealistic confidence in his or her trading ability. The unnecessary risk that the trader takes on eventually will erode the gains from the successful trades, and the trader will be back to his or her previous position, if not worse. This is an easy trap to fall into if you silence your internal prudence with arrogant and reckless overconfidence. It is essential to bear this in mind and to keep a level head so that you may listen to your self-preserving instinct and not ignore it.

The flip side of this coin is traders who turn into huge spineless pantywaists when facing the market. In this case, the trader's panic and cold feet are silencing his or her instinct. A trader who listens to internal prudence would be confident of making the right trading decisions rather than run from the markets because of some irrational and baseless fear. This may happen at the beginning for some traders who are afraid to jump into the markets. Others may face this problem after a string of losses. Whatever the reason, a trader who ignores opportunities because of fear is using emotions to dictate investing strategies and is ignoring intuition and reasoning.

Intuition and instinct also manifest themselves in the ability of a trader. That is, traders with a good intuitive feel for the markets demonstrate an intangible ability to make good trades. This can be similar to an experienced musician who does not just play a piece of music but rather makes the instrument sing. With practice, your intuition will help guide you through trades. This intuition comes with experience, where you will have the ability to process market information quickly, recognize patterns right away, and respond almost instantaneously. Intuition is not impulsive and irrational behavior but rather the result of a mature and deep understanding of how the market sentiment is moving a stock price. Trading successfully takes a mixture of art and science because the markets are driven by the reactions of human beings. The idea that having an intuitive feel for how markets react is similar to the idea that professional athletes react not only based on how a game is going but also on intangible elements such as home field advantage, momentum, and so on. Experienced traders embrace their intuition in the same way that these professional athletes do.

More important, your intuition will help you improve yourself as a trader. If you see yourself suffering a string of losses, intuitively you should be able to sense when it is not bad luck or a flawed trading strategy. Deep down, traders know when they are driving themselves to failed trades because of greed, impulsiveness, reckless behavior, hope, desire, whim, or whatever else may be driving them. The successful trader can sense that factors external to the market are driving his or her decision-making process. When this occurs, it is best to stop trading, before losses ensue, and reevaluate priorities. It is perfectly fine to not participate in the markets and to refrain from trading if you see no opportunities or if you see that you need to step back and regroup. Using the same example as earlier, coaches of professional athletes often take a time out to settle down their players and get them back on track. As a small investor, your coach is your intuition. Taking time away from trading to regroup and take stock of your positions is at times the wisest move for a trader. Your intuition is the guide that you must listen to at these moments.

Additionally, your intuition will help guide you away from unrealistic trading strategies and toward profitable investment opportunities. There is obviously a limit to how much money an individual can realistically expect to make based on how much money is available to invest initially and how much risk is tolerable. Most everyone can tell when something sounds too good to be true. If your intuition is telling you this, listen to it. Keeping your feet on the ground and knowing when you are within your limitations are essential, and you alone are in charge of doing so. It is not normal to expect to turn a $1000 investment into $100,000 trading futures in 1 year (unless you are the spouse of a prominent politician). Remember that as a direct access trader, you work your account and are solely responsible for your success or failure. Having the discipline to stick to a strategy and educating yourself about the markets are not enough. The strategy must fall in line with realistic expectations. The basic problem is that sometimes traders forget that not everyone will end up a millionaire. Extraordinary returns can only come from taking big risks—there is no free lunch. A trader expecting to make a fortune while bearing disproportionately low risk is not being realistic. Such traders are lying to themselves, ignoring their intuition, and trying to fool themselves into believing such an outcome. The basic question that occurs intuitively is, If a trading strategy yields such exceptional outcomes, why has it not occurred to others? While there is nothing wrong with striving for excellent results, the successful trader realizes that outstanding trades are infrequent. Consistency in profitable trading is what defines overall success, not enormous windfall gains. The trader can only count on himself or herself to stay out of the red and avoid second-guessing promising trading strategies because of greed, compulsion, or some self-indulgent fantasy. Fantasy is the work of theme parks; direct access traders are in the business of making profits. Your intuition is what will keep your account growing instead of shrinking from this type of unrealistic ambition. Rational investing is what will carry the day, and keeping your wits about you is the only way to avoid these unnecessary losses.

And just as some traders commit the mistake of thinking they have the magic strategy, other traders believe that they can learn a magic strategy from someone else. Nowhere does there exist an easy answer to the problem of making money. Anyone claiming that it is easy to make money on the markets has a hidden agenda, because nothing could be further from the truth. The very fact that mutual fund managers boast about beating the S&P500 is evidence enough of this. And yet people falsely claiming to know the secrets of success in the stock markets, day trading strategies, and God knows what else abound. There is an entire industry of pundits and self-described experts selling imprecise, hazy, and obscure promises of results. It is certainly untrue that everyone in the business of providing information about the stock markets and investing is a fraud. There are, in fact, many legitimate professionals who have made contributions to understanding the stock markets. Intuition will help sort out one group from the other. People who have something constructive to say generally will not need to appeal to the hopes and aspirations of the trader. They will instead appeal to the trader's rational self-interest and will say what they have to say plainly. These are professionals who are attempting to add to the knowledge of the markets. They present substantive arguments and present their work in as unambiguous a way as possible. The opposite group is made up of ineffective market pundits, self-exalting veterans, specialists, and so on. These experts are not selling investment advice as much as they are selling a fantasy to people. They tend to describe themselves more than their work. What could be more annoying than someone who states that their message is the truth because they say so and that one should believe them solely because of their credentials? Rather than making an argument on its own merits, they would have us believe that the truth flows naturally from some superior position they hold. Furthermore, they cannot sell their advice without painting rosy pictures for "Joe Sixpack" so that he believes that he can be the next Warren Buffet or George Soros. This kind of self-indulgent fantasy is only used to get money from would-be traders. Buying this kind of advice is no different from buying "get rich quick" schemes from late-night infomercials. Good advice sells itself, and the rest is entertainment. Your intuition should serve to guide you through the clutter and noise of the markets as you make the transition into direct access trading. Intuition serves the trader well in these situations. Common sense is one of the best allies of the direct access trader.

This chapter has focused on the nature of electronic direct access. Slippage and commissions are areas where direct access trading technology is superior to other forms of investing. With real-time information and instantaneous trading, direct access outperforms many other investment vehicles. The fragmented Nasdaq markets are best analyzed using this type of technology, which is perhaps why it is growing by leaps and bounds. Both small investors and big Wall Street firms are quickly adapting this new technology. The tools of direct access trading, spawned from Internet growth and day trading technology, are the most powerful tools of investing. With discipline, intuition, and a commitment to learning, the power of these tools are available for small investors to reap a greater share of the returns to their investments.

QUESTIONS

1   What are the signs that the freedom of direct access is too much
    for a small investor to handle properly before an entire nest egg has
    evaporated?

2   What are the most promising applications of direct access technol-
    ogy in terms of getting more widespread use among small investors
    beyond day traders?

3   How are brokers adapting to the environment of direct access trad-
    ing and Wall Street in general?

4   How do you control and maintain discipline throughout a trading
    frenzy?

5   What are the most effective ways of keeping oneself up to date and
    learning about new market trends?

THE GRAPEVINE

It is interesting to look at how extensive the markets have become in recent years. So many different people and institutions are investing; anyone who can get online can invest. With so many millions of distinct investors pursuing their individual goals, it would seem impossible to make heads or tails of the processes driving the markets. Some argue that this is exactly what has happened—that the markets are no longer rational and that there is no control. There still exist, however, some big signals of how the market is thinking and behaving in the aggregate. That is, even when all different kinds of people are participating in the markets, together they make up one big herd of investors. And there are ways of detecting what the herd feels like doing and which way it is likely to push prices and trading. These signals are the subject of this chapter.

Essentially, we will look at the major influences in the market. The reason we look at these is that in the past the small investor entered the markets using traditional and less efficient ways of investing, such as retail investment brokers. With these investment vehicles, small investors could only hope that the major players would not steamroll over them. Now, with the tools of direct access trading, small investors can interact in the market to prevent other players from steamrolling over them. That is, with instant order execution and real-time information, traders do not need to sit on the sidelines while price movements orchestrated by major players erode their wealth. In order to do so, and to effectively protect investment money, we will look at the major players in the market who are competing against each other and us for the funds in the market. In their drive to make money, they will attempt many different market maneuvers to make stock prices move against everyone else and in their favor. By looking at the major signals that the market has, as to its status, we can see where the players in the market are trying to move their investment dollars. Our goal is to not end up on the wrong side of the market momentum, because there is no way to fight against the current of the stock markets. Instead, we will look at the information available to investors so as to anticipate the market pressures and benefit from market momentum.

MARKET PRICES AS LEADING INDICATORS

The most important statistic in relation to any stock is its price. This number that we call *price* is what makes us or breaks us. Luckily, most of us are comfortable with the concept of prices because we encounter prices in everyday life all the time. The prices of stocks are the same as the prices of any other thing that we spend money on. Price is just the amount of money we must give up in exchange for ownership of a share of stock. The concept of prices for stock is no different from donut prices or the price of anything else. Liquidity is what sets stock apart from things like donuts. That is, that if we buy a donut, for example, we probably would have a hard time reselling it—after all, it is a used donut. If we buy stocks, however, it is not unrealistic to hope to resell the stock at a higher price.

This liquidity is what makes the markets churn out profits for investors and why many people choose to invest in stocks. As you buy, you give up money to own stock, and as you sell, you divest yourself of ownership in the stock in exchange for money. We can all agree that people investing in the stock market always prefer having more money to having less money. Hence we can agree that they would prefer to give up less money for stock, or buy at lower prices, and get more money for stock when they sell, or sell at higher prices. That is, everyone would like to buy at the lowest price possible and sell at the highest price possible. This is obviously not a groundbreaking development in finance; however, deeper below this simple concept lie some important ideas.

Suppose that a cow were to be sold. The owner could describe the weight of the cow, the cow's age, and other features perfectly. There would be no ambiguity whatsoever about the physical features of the cow. Based on these physical features, the owner may try to sell the cow at a certain price, but fundamentally, the price has nothing to do with the physical features of the cow. What the price does have to do with is how much potential buyers are interested in possessing a cow with those features. The cow is only valuable if there are people interested in buying that cow. This is a fundamental concept that drives the markets. *Nothing is of any value whatsoever unless people believe that it is valuable.* There is nothing in a pound of gold that makes it more valuable than a pound of cow dung, except that we believe that gold is more valuable. That is, we cannot measure *absolute* value; we can only measure *relative* value. In fact, in the nineteenth century, some economists tried to find some measure of absolute value, and the entire idea turned out to be an enormous dead end. Using our example, they sought some measure that would logically dictate that a pound of gold is more valuable than a pound of cow dung, but none exists. Only in our minds is gold more valuable than cow dung.

In the markets, all prices are relative. A stock is only valuable when there are buyers and sellers ready to support its price. Thus, for example, Motorola will only sell at 180 if there are buyers standing ready to pay $180 per share. If people are only willing to pay $170 per share, the bid will become 170. The same goes for the offer. If no one is offering Motorola shares for less than $180, then the stock will only be available at 180. Only if people are willing to offer their shares for less, say, 170, will the offer fall to 170.

Thus, in determining the price of stocks, there are two opposing forces that every individual faces. The first is the desire to make the most money from the stock. This leads to trying to buy stock at the lowest price possible or trying to sell the stock at the highest price possible. The second, or opposing force, is that whenever you attempt to sell or buy, someone must take the opposite side of the trade. That is, if you wish to realize a trade at a certain price, someone else must wish to trade the stock with you at that price. If you are selling, for example, you may push for a high ask price, but you must temper your efforts because no one may wish to buy from you at a high price. If no one is buying, you will have to either sell at a lower price or not sell at all. This is important because you must keep in mind that whenever a trade is executed, both parties believe that the price of the trade is the best price they can get at that moment. If one of the two believes that he or she can do better, he or she will not trade at that price but at the better price. And most important, one of the two parties is wrong. No seller intentionally sells if it is known that the price will increase, because the seller can just wait a moment and sell at a higher price. Equivalently, no buyer will buy knowing that the price will decrease, because the buyer can wait a moment and buy at a lower price. Thus the stock markets are a place where people are betting on which way the price will move on a stock, and half the people trading are always on the wrong side of the price movement.

BEARS AND BULLS

As mentioned in Chapter 2, the movements in stock prices are described using two particular animals. They are the bear and the bull. Recall that a *bear market* is a market in which prices are falling. We also can say that investors are *bearish* on a stock if the investors are selling the stock short in anticipation of the price falling. To say that a market is bearish is to say that people are agreeing that the price of a stock is becoming less valuable. In these markets, buyers benefit from cheaper stock prices, whereas sellers, who like to sell at high prices, are giving in. This is why the price is falling. Sellers are faced with the following dilemma: They wish to sell, but they also wish to get high prices. In a bear market, the seller's need to get a high price is not as important as the need to sell. The seller has a greater desire to fill that order than to force the buyer to pay a higher price. Equivalently, the bear market buyer is aware of buying into a falling market. The bear market buyer faces the opposite tradeoff that the seller faces. The buyer can demand a lower price but risks not finding a seller. In a bear market, the buyer's ability to demand lower prices and find someone willing to sell at the lower price is enhanced. The fundamental idea is that since prices are falling in a bear market, it is better to be selling than to be buying, so buyers demand a cheaper price as compensation for taking the less advantageous position.

Remember, however, that no one is forcing anyone's hand here. If sellers are allowing the price to fall, we must assume that it is in their best interest to do so, given the prevailing market conditions. The price in the market is being decided in a game of tug of war between buyers and sellers. If sellers are ceding to buyers in terms of prices, they are doing so because they see opportunity in selling. This is what defines a bearish trader. The trader who is bearish is willing to sell at the lower price, betting that it will continue to fall. A trader who sells a stock short, as the price falls, makes more money. Everyone selling on the way down is making money, except for the last person who sold. The last seller is left holding the bag, having sold stock at its cheapest price. The last bearish trader to sell is betting that the price will continue to fall, and it does not. The last seller has sold the stock at the lowest possible price. At this point, since prices stop falling, the momentum swings to buyers. Up to this point, sellers are willing to sell at lower and lower prices because they believe the prices will fall even more and they can buy back what they sold at cheaper prices. Momentum swings when prices get so low that sellers back out of the market unless they can get a higher price.

In the markets, everything happens for a reason. When prices in a bear market stop falling, it is because buyers are not demanding cheaper prices to buy. Sellers are less willing to lower their prices, and buyers must pay more. At this point we say that the market has turned *bullish*. In other words, a market in which prices are increasing is called a *bull market*. What characterizes a bull market is that in the tug of war over prices between buyers and sellers, the sellers begin to pull harder. Recall the tradeoff of sellers, who try to sell at the highest prices possible but must find someone willing to buy at high prices. Buyers, equivalently, face the tradeoff of trying to buy at the lowest prices but must find someone willing to sell to them at these lower prices. When in a bull market, buyers relax their demands for lower prices in order to buy. Buyers push the stock price up because they are more willing to pay a higher price, even though they would prefer not to. In this situation, people are willing to pay higher prices because they think that the price increases will continue after they own the stock. Buyers feel that the opportunity to own stock in the increasing market is worth the higher price. It is because of this that sellers can get the stock price to increase. They can demand a higher price, and someone will come forward and pay it. In a bull market, since prices are increasing, sellers hold the upper hand. It is their position that is increasing in value, and hence they can command a higher price.

The parallel argument about the interests of buyers applies in this situation. Buyers will not pay a higher price out of the goodness of their hearts. A buyer will pay a higher price in the belief that buying into an increasing market is his or her best move. The seller will sell because of the belief that it is a good time to relinquish ownership of the stock. The increase in prices will continue so long as the bullish buyers are willing to pay higher prices. The moment buyers see that prices have gone so high that they cannot possibly continue to increase, they will no longer be willing to pay high prices. Buyers know that finding someone to sell to will be impossible at a price higher than they paid when the time to resell comes.

Note that as prices are moving due to the pressure of market participants who are either bearish or bullish on the stocks, they have one of four basic motivations for buying and selling:

Reasons for buying
1   Take the long position—buying for bullish reasons
2   Cover a short position—buying back stock previously sold for bearish reasons

Reasons for selling
1   Take a short position—selling stock in anticipation of price fall, bearish
2   Close out a long position—selling a stock bought previously for bullish reasons

Notice the second reason for buying. If prices are increasing and people are covering their shorts, they are losing money with every teenie increase in the prices. These individuals will be buying aggressively because they need to get out of their short position to limit their losses. Recall that these individuals are in the position of having sold the stock without owning it. If prices increase, they must replace the stock at a higher price and take a loss. As a result, their efforts at buying back the stock quickly to limit their losses may push up the prices in a much more dramatic way than if people were just buying to take the long position. The desperation of such buyers can make the increase in prices very sharp.

A similar situation can arise with respect to the second reason for selling. If prices are falling and people are closing out their long positions, they will sell aggressively in order to escape a bad trade. They own the stock and are watching its value decline, so they may panic and sell. This type of frantic selling may further cause a price fall. These declines are much more violent than the opposite situation, where people are taking profits as prices increase.

This type of phenomenon works like a snowball effect, where price momentum gets stronger and stronger. Two important results arise from these momentum swings. The first is that most of the time, strong stocks tend to get stronger, and weak stocks tend to get weaker. The second is that as traders get caught up in the market frenzy, they miss the turning points. When momentum swings, they may miss the signs. One of the most obvious signs that prices are going to change direction is if they reach a level where they previously changed direction. That is, if prices are falling, they may begin to increase again at a level where they stopped falling previously on other declines. The level where prices stop falling and increase is called the *support*. Analogously, if prices are increasing, they may stop increasing and begin to fall again at a certain price level, where during previous rallies the price stopped increasing. This price level is called the *resistance*. The support and resistance levels work like psychological price floors and price ceilings. Thus, for example, as a stock price falls, many investors may have sold the stock short, and they may expect the price to rebound when it hits the support level. As the stock price reaches the support level, these investors rush to buy, to cover their shorts, and they push the price back up, thereby reinforcing the support. Similarly, if a price is increasing, many investors may be long on the stock, and once it reaches the resistance level, they may sell out their long positions because they fear the price will fall. As investors are eager to sell to take profits, they may push the price back down, thereby reinforcing the resistance.

INFORMATION AND INFLUENCE

By nature of the Nasdaq markets, trading absolutely requires having as much information about what is going on as possible. As we have seen, the Nasdaq markets are extremely fractured and decentralized. Participants from all parts of the country are trading from their computers or trading terminals. And the market prices depend on what all the participants at their different computer terminals are doing as a whole. That is, the aggregate trading decisions of the market participants directly determine prices. If, for example, everyone believes that the stock price is going up, then as a result of this belief, there may emerge a bullish demand for the stock. The stock's price will increase accordingly as many bullish traders become more willing to pay higher prices to buy. Hence the willingness to pay higher prices is based on the group's bullish beliefs that prices will increase. These beliefs themselves drive the prices up. As a result, this type of trading environment functions on self-fulfilling situations. Because of this, it is important to see what factors affect how the group as a whole forms its beliefs. That is, the herd of traders drives the market prices, and the herd of traders is driven by information about the markets. For this reason, we need to know as much about what information is reaching market participants as possible. We need to know how the herd will react to information to know how prices will react.

As the herd receives information, they are receiving a picture of the market, the relative interest in stocks, the possible changes in market activity, and so on. Essentially, since the market is composed of so many different kinds of buyers and sellers and there is so much going on simultaneously, what traders search for in market information is a big picture. Traders look to market information for some sort of a bird's eye view of where buying and selling pressure is. They look for a way to both summarize the activity and systematize the changes in order to decide if they should buy, sell, or do nothing. In order to make these decisions, market information is disseminated by many different sources.

These sources of information are simply the voices of different market participants, however. That is, traders on the Nasdaq all take their information and signals from a few institutions and market participants who have the power and influence to reach the general participants. When these powerful institutions disseminate their opinions about the market, these opinions reach everyone through different media that shall be discussed, e.g., the financial press and others. What is important for now is that since market information is driving prices and people disseminating information are participating in the markets themselves, then we can assume that these people will use their influence in the market to move prices in a direction that is favorable to them. That is, since they have a vested interest in how the prices will move, the institutions in the market that have the power to describe the market conditions to other traders will do so in a way that is favorable to their own market position. Since they know that they serve as the eyes and ears of traders, inasmuch as they can, they will describe a picture of the markets that will move prices toward their strategic market interests. The picture of the markets that these powerful influences give us need not be absolutely the most objective market picture because, as we have seen, the markets are based on what people believe, not what is going on. If enough people believe that what is being described to them is the true market situation, it becomes the true market situation. This self-fulfilling market behavior gives the newsmakers leeway in reporting their opinion about the markets. If they can convince enough participants of their opinion, then their opinion becomes the prevailing market mood. That is, through dissemination of market information, the powerful institutions on Wall Street can steer the herd of traders toward a picture of the market that is convenient for them.

This is not to say that the information in the financial press is a complete ploy to redirect markets and has no basis in reality. The news, in order to effectively move markets, must be credible to traders. Thus financial information must reflect the reality of the markets in some measure in order to preserve its usefulness to its audience. In this situation, reputation can be very important in deciding whether to give the market new information. As we shall see, the most important issue regarding new information is knowing how the market will react. Moreover, by knowing the incentives of the influential market agents disseminating the news, we can understand the direction in which they are attempting to drive market prices.

The most informative item of market information available about a stock is the company's earnings report. This is like the company's report card; it comes out every quarter and reports the company's earnings per share, its revenues, and other relevant market information about that quarter's performance. Since the earnings report tells of the success or failure of a company in the marketplace in terms of profits, it is the most closely watched information about a company. Managers and officers of publicly traded companies are aware of this and know that the value of their portfolio can change dramatically as earnings reports become public information. These managers have the inside track on the companies and know if the earnings reports will live up to market expectations or will fail to meet market expectations. This information can be extremely valuable. A chief executive officer (CEO) who knows that the company's earnings report will fail to meet market expectations also knows that the stock price will fall. As a result, the CEO has an incentive to sell early.

Equivalently, if the company's earnings will exceed market expectations, the stock price will increase because the company will be seen as surprisingly profitable. As a result, if earnings will come in better than expected, company insiders may buy stock before the earnings report becomes public. This type of buying and selling on private company information is called *insider trading* and is illegal. It is, however, impossible to prevent. While it is illegal for a CEO to purchase stock on inside information, who is to say that close friends of the CEO cannot purchase stock before earnings reports become public? It is impossible to know if the CEO has advised these close friends about the buying opportunity based on inside information. For this reason, it is impossible to prevent insider trading. Since it is impossible to prevent and there is an incentive for agents with inside information to buy or sell early, then we can observe early buying and selling of the stock to forecast the earnings reports. That is, in the days and weeks before a company publishes its earnings report, if there is increased buying in the stock, it may be due to insiders buying into the company before good news is released and the stock price increases. If people know that the earnings will be better than expected and that the price will increase, it is likely that they seize on the buying opportunity. As they buy, they are indicating to the market that the information about to be released will be good news. The opposite situation need not be true. While people have an incentive to sell when they know that the earnings will disappoint the market expectations, they also sell at times when they need money. That is, the fact that stock is being sold does not always imply that someone thinks that the stock price will fall, because the seller may need cash and is selling the stock to get it. Since there is no need to buy stock similar to the need to have money, buying is a more informational transaction. In other words, people may sell because they need the money, regardless of whether the price will fall or not, whereas no one buys because they *need* to own the stock.

Analyst expectations are also extremely influential in moving the price of a stock. I mentioned analyst expectations in previous chapters. Recall that analysts are individuals hired by large brokerage houses to track stocks and try to anticipate what earnings and company performance will be. The most interesting characteristic about analyst expectations is that when they are taken in consensus, they are believed to be one of the most important leading indicators of how a company will perform. Thus, for example, suppose that there were only two analysts for Microsoft and their average earnings prediction was $0.70 per share. In this example, the market consensus for earnings in the coming quarter would be $0.70, and supposedly, Microsoft's earnings should come in at or very close to $0.70 per share. This type of prediction of a company's earnings is calculated four times a year and is often revised by analysts as new information becomes available.

In order to calculate their earnings expectations, analysts look at different kinds of information that could influence a company's profitability. They may look at not only information specific to the firm that has emerged since the last report but also new information regarding the firm's competitors. They may look at macroeconomic variables, and in addition, analysts may have inside or private information about the companies from close relationships with the company officers or other sources. Studies on the accuracy of these forecasts have found that analysts outperform mechanical models in prediction, but only insofar as they can get inside information. As more firm-specific information becomes available to them, they are better able to predict the earnings.

It is interesting to note that the consensus analyst expectation is a weighted average of all the expectations of the analysts following a certain stock. In a way, earnings expectations serve as a sort of benchmark for the performance of a company. If a company fails to meet them, the company's management is viewed as underperforming, not the analysts. This is like a weather forecaster predicting sun, and when it rains, people blaming nature for not meeting the weather forecaster's expectations. What is interesting is that this phenomenon gives analysts the power to influence stock prices through their expectations. It is well known that if an analyst gives a sell recommendation, a stock price generally falls. It is this type of influence on a stock price that can give analysts strong influences over market prices and influence in driving the herd of investors toward where they wish them to be.

We can look at an extreme example of the power of earnings expectations over stock prices that occurred in the markets. Procter and Gamble (P&G), a large producer of consumer products such as Tide detergent and Pampers diapers, a solid and profitable blue chip company, should not and usually does not have a very volatile stock price. Early in March of 2000, however, the company announced that it expected third-quarter earnings per share (EPS) to be about 10 percent below the previous year's EPS. Analysts had expected earnings to be at about $0.78 per share, and the company announced that earnings were going to be more on the order of $0.65 per share. This failure to meet expectations led to an enormous

1-day sell-off of P&G. On volume of over 68 million shares, the stock price plunged by more than $30 per share before somewhat recovering and ended down 31 percent on the day. The case of P&G shows the extent to which not meeting analysts' expectations can cause a company to fall out of favor with market investors.

The analysts predicting earnings and following stocks work for large brokerage houses and investment firms on Wall Street. This employment situation gives rise to a conflict of interest, in that analysts obviously have the power to influence stock prices through their earnings reports and recommendations; however, to maintain any semblance of credibility, these reports and recommendations are supposed to represent impartial analysis of a company's future prospects. Yet the analysts issuing these reports are working for brokerage firms. These firms may have large holdings in the stocks that these individuals are analyzing, and some would even argue that it is in the best interest of the firms to hold the stock that their analysts follow. How impartial can analysts be if their employer stands to lose or gain depending on the outcome of their analysis? This situation is analogous to McGraw-Hill having a specialist in finance books on the payroll critiquing this book. To say the least, the critic would have an incentive to be kind in his or her evaluation. Similarly, we would all like to hear the opinion of a professional analyst who is following a company 24 hours a day; however, the salary of such an analyst is paid by a Wall Street firm. This firm, like all investors, stands to benefit tremendously if it can sway market opinion in favor of its investment positions. Insofar as the analyst who works for it sways the market, the firm is able to do just that. As long as a vestige of credibility can be maintained, the analyst can move stock prices through his or her expectations reports.

Suppose, for example, that some large Wall Street firm believes that some company in which it is long has good potential. Suppose we call it the ZZZ Company. That is, the Wall Street firm owns a lot of ZZZ stock and would like to see the value increase. If the Wall Street firm is looking to sell off a large block of the stock, it would like to do so without causing the price to fall so that it can take maximum profits. Either way, it would be to the benefit of the Wall Street firm to see the stock price increase. Now, suppose that the firm has an analyst who follows ZZZ. The Wall Street firm could sit back and sell off its block of ZZZ stock, hoping that its market maker can do a good job dumping all the stock without too much of a price fall. On the other hand, the Wall Street firm could call up its analyst and tell him or her to set low earnings expectations for ZZZ. If the analyst does so, ZZZ is sure to beat the expectations, and the stock price will increase. Additionally, with low expectations, the analyst can revise his or her expectations upward and draw attention to ZZZ as a good buy. All these maneuvers allow the Wall Street firm to sell large blocks of the stock without the price falling because it is generating interest in ZZZ.

There is an analogous scenario for the case where the Wall Street firm wishes to buy the stock or wishes to see the stock price fall. Suppose the Wall Street firm is planning to buy a large number of ZZZ shares. One alternative is to give the order to its market maker and let the chips fall where they may. In this case, the market maker will endeavor to buy the large number of shares without running up the price too much. The other alternative for the Wall Street firm is to employ all the resources at its disposal (i.e., all the employees on its payroll) by using the power of its analyst. If the analyst for the firm following ZZZ stock revises expectations downward, the market will look unfavorably on ZZZ Company. If the analyst sets high earnings expectations, ZZZ will most likely be unable to hit the figure, and the market will look on ZZZ as failing to reach its potential. The market will look to sell ZZZ because of its inability to make its expected earnings. Either move gives the Wall Street firm the needed selling interest in the market for it to buy.

We may ask ourselves whether this type of attempt at manipulating the markets makes sense for a Wall Street firm. That is, there certainly exists the potential for this activity to occur, but it will most likely occur if it is in the best interest of the Wall Street firm to go ahead with it. The profit motive is undoubtedly there. Insofar as the big Wall Street firms control the movements of the markets, they control how their profits are made and can reduce uncertainty and losses. Looking at the other side of the coin, what other incentive would a Wall Street firm have to publish its salaried employees' research besides working the market sentiment? Certainly, if the analyst for ZZZ knew that something spectacular was about to occur, what incentive would the firm have to release that information? The point of predicting earnings is to have the information early, before the rest of the market finds out how a company's profits are. However, if these forecasts were dead accurate, why would a company release them to the public? If Wall Street analysts knew ahead of time about spectacular price movements from their forecasts, they could be the first to take positions in the market. One can only assume, then, that the information they release as forecasted earnings is designed to influence the market sentiment about the stocks.

The point here is not to promote distrust in market analysts, because trusting or not trusting is beside the point. Rather, one should abstract from the issue of whether their information is genuine and look at which way these analysts are trying to push the stock. For example, if analysts downgrade a stock or give a sell recommendation, a sell-off almost surely will ensue, regardless of the company's fundamentals. When this type of recommendation is given, analysts are revealing that they want a sell-off to occur in the stock or, at the very least, are already prepared for one. In this case, Wall Street may be covering its shorts or looking to take a long position in the stock. And it often will be more than one firm's analyst who may downgrade a stock. Furthermore, it is not unreasonable to expect analysts in different firms to back each other's recommendations to maintain the strength of their ability to move markets. As Benjamin Franklin said, we must hang together, or we will surely all hang separately. If analyst recommendations are to move markets, the consensus market opinion must credibly predict earnings. If all analysts say sell and the public sells, the analysts maintain their credibility. If one does not say sell and the price falls because all the others do, the analyst comes out looking bad. If there is dissension among all of them, the public does not know what to believe, and they all lose their ability to sway markets as expectations lose their forecasting value. For this reason, it is in the best interest of analysts to extend professional courtesies to each other and hang together, so to speak.

So far we have seen market information available from companies themselves, as well as analysts. These are the most direct market signals for stocks because they move stock prices day in and day out. There are other sources of information, however, that periodically emerge and can affect stock prices to varying degrees. Remember, however, that we look at this information because we can see what big players in the market are doing by how the information they are releasing is supposed to affect market prices. Thus, for example, if they are pushing prices up, they must be trying to sell, and if they are pushing prices down, they must be buying. As they try to push stocks in one direction or another, we can see where the smart money on Wall Street is betting. These big firms are not the only source of information, however. Some others follow.

There are many kinds of market news reports available. Some, such as *Investor's Business Daily,* the *Wall Street Journal,* "Nightly Business

Report," CNBC, "Bloomberg," and others, are comprehensive financial news sources. These newspapers and news programs go over important events relating to companies, such as court decisions, merger announcements, strikes, political events, etc. They are important sources of information because what they report is considered to be the most broad-based public information available. That is, once the *Wall Street Journal* reports some news about a company, we can assume that everyone interested in that stock has that information. Furthermore, these news sources will give the news the appropriate spin and basically analyze what the effect of the news is expected to be in the market. The news reports establish what the market reaction to the news should be.

News reports can have a very powerful effect on a company's stock price not only because they bring the most recent information to the market but also because they can trigger latent anxiety in the market about a stock or group. That is, a big news report can affect a stock and other related stocks in a very strong way because it gives investors the excuse that they were looking for to turn bullish or bearish on the stocks. For example, in late 1999 and the early part of 2000, a mood set in among some investors that the technology stocks may be overvalued. Then, in the early part of April 2000, after the regular market session closed, a federal judge found that Microsoft had violated antitrust law. Microsoft, the software giant, fell over 15 points to 90⅞. With more than $5 billion in shares outstanding, the tumble in its stock price shaved nearly $80 billion off the company's market capitalization. The news of the ruling began a wave of technology sell-offs as investors punished the entire technology sector. The Nasdaq Composite Index, which had lost nearly 400 points the previous week, fell 349.15 points, or 7.64 percent. Investors ran from technology, as was evident in the Dow Jones Industrial Average (DJIA). Even though the DJIA includes Microsoft among its 30 components, it put on a solid rally, gaining 300.01 points, or 2.75 percent, on the day. In terms of points, the gain was the sixth largest on record for the Dow. For the Nasdaq, it was the fifth largest decline in percentage terms and the largest drop ever in points.

This example illustrates two important market characteristics that are observable as news is revealed. The first deals with the behavior of stock prices after news is revealed. We should expect that as the news of the ruling against Microsoft spreads, people will want to sell off the stock. That is, if the government is succeeding in its antitrust case, the ramifications threaten the profitability of Microsoft and introduce more uncertainty with respect to ownership of that company. As a result, it is reasonable to expect that people will want to sell off some of their holdings of Microsoft. In this case, the price should fall as the market for Microsoft turns bearish, which is what occurred. This, however, is not the only possible outcome. It is often the case that an announcement such as this one produces the opposite effect. That is, an announcement is made from which one would expect the stock price to fall, and the stock price does not fall. A classic example of this is when the Federal Reserve increases interest rates, and the market does not fall, but rather increases. We would expect stock prices to move in one direction, and they move the opposite way. The reason for this is that individuals anticipate the announcement accurately, and they incorporate the forthcoming news into their buying positions. Then the news comes as no surprise to anyone, and it confirms the expectations of individuals. What happens then is that the markets may have expected the price to fall, and many individuals may have taken the short position. When the price does not fall, because the news came as no surprise to anyone, individuals with short positions must rush to cover their shorts. As they are forced to buy back stocks, they push the price up instead of down. The analogous case would be an announcement from which everyone anticipates the price to increase, and when the news breaks, the price does not increase. As people try to get out of the stock, they push the price down; instead of increasing the price, the announcement causes the price to fall.

The second market characteristic that is illustrated in the sharp Microsoft decline has to do with the stock groups or market sectors. When an announcement has a strong effect on a stock, the effect carries over to similar stocks or stocks in the same sector. In this case, Microsoft was the bellwether of computer technology stocks. The Nasdaq computer composite index took a dive right behind Microsoft. Bad news for a prominent stock can spark a sell-off in many similar stocks. The performance leading indicators such as Microsoft can set the mood for the sector and for the market as a whole. Hence, if an announcement is made about a sector leader, the effect of the announcement will be felt across that sector.

Beyond specific announcements that are made by some company in particular, there are many important indicators about the performance of the stock market that are relevant. The Federal Reserve (abbreviated Fed), which is the central bank for the government of the United States, sets the discount rate for banks, which is roughly the cost of doing business

for banks in the United States. As they raise the discount rate, they force
banks to lend less, and hence they slow down the economy. When the
Fed raises the discount rate, it is announcing to the financial community
that it is the intention of the central bank to slow down the economy
before inflation sets in. Usually the markets anticipate what the Fed's
increases in the discount rate will be. If the markets anticipate the increases accurately, then stock prices do not fall, but if the Fed raises the
discount rate more than expected, the markets are shocked and decline.

Financial news programs can be of use to keep up on what has occurred throughout the day, but generally lots of people have access to the
information being reported before it is actually broadcast. For this reason,
it is better to look at this type of information as useful for deciphering
the mood of the markets than as a place for good stock tips. Sometimes
financial news programs have guests who work in the markets giving their
opinions and analysis on the current market conditions as well. These
individuals may be successful mutual fund managers, pension fund managers, or asset managers for insurance companies, for example. They may
be asked to appear on the programs because they stand out as authorities
in one market sector or because they have a good record for picking
stocks. Their advice, however, suffers from the same problem as that of
the analysts. They have absolutely no real incentive to give out good stock
picks; rather, what they do have an incentive to do is try to move markets
to benefit themselves. They may, for example, have some "dog" stock
that they need to get off their hands and will publicize it as a buying
opportunity with "real growth potential" just to generate enough interest
for them to sell out their positions at a decent price. What is in their best
interest to do is to publicize stocks in which they have a long position
and to suggest that the stocks in which they have short positions are not
a good buy. This is irrelevant to whether these stocks really are good or
bad buys. If the publicity works, it will be a good buy for the money
managers, which is what is important for them and what will make their
record look good.

The Standard & Poors 500 (S&P500), which is the market portfolio,
the Dow Jones Industrial Average, and the Nasdaq Composite Index are
the main indicators of market performance. These are extremely useful
for detecting how the market is doing. They serve as a measure of the
general market. They serve as a benchmark for how a stock is performing
throughout the day. For example, bullish investors may push a stock up
on some given day, while the S&P500 is down and beginning to recover.

As the S&P500 increases, the strong stock should get stronger still. Equivalently, if a stock is underperforming and the market takes a downturn, the weak stock should continue down as the market goes down. The market pushes stocks in its direction, and the way to observe which way the market is moving is mainly the Nasdaq Composite and the S&P500. The Nasdaq Composite is important because it is like the average performance of the stocks that electronic direct access traders mainly trade, i.e., Nasdaq stocks. The S&P500 is important because it is an excellent leading indicator of general economic activity for the United States and is closely watched by all traders. The Dow Jones Industrial Average contains the 30 largest and most influential companies in the United States. It is a useful index to watch; however, it has shown an increasing tendency to move against the Nasdaq Composite. That is, the DJIA and the Nasdaq Composite have been moving in opposite directions more and more. Furthermore, the DJIA represents more stable companies and may not pick up the volatility of the Nasdaq markets. The Nasdaq, however, is still strongly influenced by the DJIA. Investors sometimes flee from one market to the other; i.e., they flee from the Nasdaq markets to the New York Stock Exchange, so the DJIA remains an important indicator for market performance.

Besides the market portfolios, government statistics are useful to look at, in that they capture the underlying fundamental characteristics of the economic activity. The big money on Wall Street keeps a close eye on these figures in order to decide where to invest, so such statistics can be very influential in the stock markets. These statistics are reported in the financial press, such as the *Wall Street Journal.* Each Saturday, *Barron's* gives a list of important figures that will be released by the government in the following week. Some important statistics are the consumer price index and the producer price index because these give a measure of inflation. This means that they describe how quickly prices are increasing. It is the Fed's job to fight inflation, so the more price indexes are increasing, the more the Fed has an incentive to raise interest rates and hence lower stock prices. Unemployment figures and productivity figures are also important because if unemployment is very low, then companies have to raise salaries to induce people to come work for them. This situation is called a *tight labor market,* and the Fed does not like it because higher wages lead to higher prices and to inflation. Productivity figures are important because they reflect how much people are able to produce at their jobs. If people produce a lot, then paying workers more is not inflationary. If productivity is high, companies can pay workers higher salaries, and the Fed should not be concerned with greater inflation.

Some other statistics that guide investors are bond yields and short interests. *Bond yields* are the returns to savings bonds. Bonds are a safer alternative to investing in stocks. For investors, bonds represent the trade-off of receiving a lower return but at lower risk. Essentially, bonds serve as a loan that one makes to the government or a corporation, for example. The investor pays the bond price, and the government uses that money for 10 or 30 years and may pay a fixed amount every year to the owner of the bond as interest. While the amount paid either yearly or at expiration is fixed, the price of the bond fluctuates all the time. As the bond price increases, the bond yield falls, because you get the same fixed payment but it costs more to get it, hence a lower yield. If the government sees that there is too much inflation, it decreases bond prices so that the interest rate, or bond yield, increases, and the economy slows down. The problem for investors is basically that bond prices and interest rates are like opposite ends of a seesaw. The higher the interest rate, the lower is the bond price. If there is inflation, people fear that bond prices will fall. For this reason, investors look at bond yields. *Short interest* refers to a listing of how much stock of each company has been sold short by investors. Short interest serves as a measure of whether the market feels that stock prices will fall. The short interest lists appear in the *Wall Street Journal, Barron's, Investors Business Daily,* and so on. Short interest is useful because if many people sold a stock short, they will need to cover their shorts in the event that the price begins to increase, which will further push the price up. If there is a lot of short interest in a stock that is falling, when it reaches the support level, all these people will likely buy to take profits, and this will push the stock price right back up. For these reasons, investors keep an eye on short interest.

Further sources of information on the market for investors are publications such as investment newsletters, investment columns in newspapers, and other random sources of investment advice, market critiques and forecasts, and so on. These kinds of investment news sources differ from other sources in that they are not as publicized or do not have as large an audience as some of the larger financial news venues. It is best to be very wary of the informational content of these reports. Some can be helpful to certain kinds of investors because they provide market-neutral information, such as investment-related tax advice or very basic information designed to introduce beginners to the markets. These may explain different options available to beginning investors, places to look for information, and so on. Other columns or advisors suggest to investors where the smart money on Wall Street is investing and may make all kinds of forecasts as to where the markets are going. Again, the basic problem with these kinds of forecasts is that if they were accurate, their informational content would be invaluable and certainly would not be published. If they were forecasts designed to sway the public toward a position favorable to the forecaster, then there would be a rational motive for their publication. But even if the readers of these investment circulars did buy the forecasts contained in them, the circulation is too small and insignificant to move the markets. Hence the publisher cannot realistically expect that putting out this information will generate sufficient interest in one stock or another. Instead, these publishers may be putting out this information for two other reasons. The first is that they may make money selling investors on the idea of having privileged information. They present investors with the false opportunity of being inside the Wall Street loop. This is unrealistic; it is naive to believe that a publication would give out any information that would reveal what Wall Street insiders may be thinking. If people believe that this is what they are getting, however, these publications can make sales or generate advertisement revenue based on their circulation. The second reason that these kinds of investment recommendations and forecasts are published is simply for the publicity it generates. Just the fact that an individual is consulted for forecasts and investment tips is good advertising for his or her ability and, perhaps, investment consulting services. Even in the case where the individuals giving out the advice would want to come off as excellent forecasters, they will still not have any incentive to give out their stock advice. After all, why buy the cow when you can get the milk for free? In this case, why pay for investment advice from an excellent forecaster when you can just read an advertising letter and get the advice for free? Furthermore, if the investment advice is so great, why would they sell their services to us and not to Warren Buffet, who would most likely be willing to pay more for it?

Economists often joke that they do not answer questions because they know the answer but because they are asked. There may be some uneasy truth in this joke when considering forecasts of the stock market as well. No one knows what the stock market will do. While it may be reassuring to hear forecasts that, if they come true, would imply big profits for one's current positions, there is limited value in these forecasts. A forecast is one possible outcome of many that could occur in the future. If it is a good forecast, then there is a high probability that what is predicted actually occurs. However, it is only one outcome that could occur, and we should consider all the possible contingencies. For this reason, it is best to not invest as if the forecast were going to happen but rather as if the forecast may happen, and if it does not, then your positions should not be worthless. This is especially true considering that the forecasts that are freely available are not the highest-probability ones or the most accurate ones. For example, forecasters love to use the same old trick of giving a figure but not a date or a date but not a figure. In this way they can never get pinned down as being inaccurate. For example, one forecaster may forecast that the S&P500 will pull back by 5 percent in the future. What does this mean? Eventually, the S&P500 will have a 5 percent pullback, but this could be in 20 years or after it increases by 700 percent based on this forecast. Another may say that the biotechnology sector is showing growth potential in the next 2 months. Could these forecasts be any more ambiguous? Yet they are published all the time. Another trick that forecasters use is a basic application of the law of large numbers. They bang out dozens of forecasts, and sooner or later, one comes close to reality. Buying or selling a stock short because, based on a forecast, you anticipate a price change is a very risky business. Instead, look to the market pressures that brought the stock to where it is, and consider the likelihood of the market pressure turning bearish or bullish on the stock. Trying to predict where the stock will be on some future date is like trying to spot a firefly sitting on the edge of a spotlight. Instead, ignore insignificant forecasts, and look to the market participants to see who is looking to sell, who is looking to buy, and where the prices are likely to change direction as the mood turns bearish or bullish.

This chapter looked at two central influences in the market, the prices and the information disseminated about how these prices are and may be moving. We saw the arbitrary nature of pricing and how market pressure can move it one way or the other. We then saw the different informational media by which large players try to influence the market-wide thinking of investors so as to move prices to profitable positions. The next chapter examines the specific goals and incentives some of the major players themselves have. We will put ourselves in the place of the major investors on Wall Street. By looking at the motivations and the different kinds of major players, we can learn to spot where they are moving the market to and profit from these moves. We look at the incentives of major players in the market to see where they will put pressure on prices. Knowing this, we can make sure that we do not end up on the wrong side of the price movements that they bring about.

QUESTIONS

1   If market participants push prices and prices draw market participants, when does this process become too unstable for one to trade successfully for profit?

2   Do people trading in the markets believe that stocks have some intrinsic price based on the company reputation and that prices will in the long run revert to this value?

3   How does the battle between bears and bulls develop throughout the trading day? Does the small investor figure in at all?

4   Is it profitable for the small investor to try to jump into the fight between the bears and the bulls?

5   When, if ever, is the fluctuation of prices too much for short selling?

7

THE PLAYERS

The markets that we invest in are made up of a series of different individuals who have access to different amounts of money to invest and different intentions and goals for their investment dollars. In previous chapters we have seen how the tools of direct access trading are allowing small investors access to these markets and how the markets move as a whole. This chapter looks at the major categories of investors and market participants against whom the small investor is trading in the markets.

MARKET MAKERS

Previously, I defined *market makers* as the group of market participants who represent financial institutions in the Nasdaq markets and are collectively responsible for providing liquidity to stocks traded on the Nasdaq exchanges. Recall that to provide liquidity simply means that there must always be a buying and selling presence in the markets for all the actively traded stocks. Thus, when market makers are fulfilling their role as providers of liquidity, they are buying or selling from other market participants and ensuring that there is always a party present in the markets who is ready to buy or sell. This role is important because it gives everyone investing in the markets the security of knowing that all it takes to withdraw their money from an investment is to access the markets' trade. There will always be a presence standing ready to buy or sell from investors. Of course, recall that market makers are allowed to charge a spread so that they can profit from their role as providers of liquidity. Furthermore, recall that market makers always must be present at the bid or ask price; they cannot back away if they do not feel like trading. If they did, the other market makers would ostracize them. This is a very important characteristic, which I will refer to later. Providing liquidity, however, is not their only role in the investment world.

A second function of market makers is to trade for their high-volume clients. Large corporations and institutional clients such as pension funds, banks, and others who have a lot of trading volume turn to big Wall Street firms for their investments. These firms handle these large accounts through their market makers, reaping large commissions through the sheer volume of trading of their larger clients. The market makers who handle these large trades must earn their commissions by using every means at their disposal to ensure that their clients get the best possible prices. Essentially, large clients are willing to pay big commissions so long as the savings from getting good prices on their large-volume transactions outweigh the cost of these commissions. As a result, it is important for the market makers to secure good prices for the large clients of the brokerage house that employs them. Furthermore, these clients are scrutinizing the performance of the market makers based on an average price for that day, called the *value-weighted average price* (VWAP). This is the yardstick used to measure the effectiveness of market makers in securing good prices for their clients. This statistic captures the mean price at which most of the quantity of stock trades each day. This can be very influential in the behavior of a market maker because a market maker who is not beating the VWAP has an incentive to force the price toward the desired level. That is, toward the end of the trading day, market makers sometimes must push stock prices artificially high or low just to get the average to where they do not look bad in the eyes of their clients because they performed up to par with the VWAP.

The third function of market makers is to take speculative positions of their own with the inventory of stock they maintain. That is, market makers keep an account with stock in it, which they sometimes sell to their clients. At other times, however, the market makers should use that stock, and also take short positions if they do not own stock, to make money off the markets. Because they maintain a presence in the markets at all times, market makers are constantly watching stock price movements and are very aware of the trading activity. Furthermore, they know all the publicly available information about the markets and also have their own private order flow. When they have a large buy order, they know that they will have to push prices up, for example. This sort of information is the most lucrative kind to possess. With this kind of information, it is only natural that market makers actively trade with their accounts and take positions throughout the trading day.

Recall the media that market makers use to conduct their trading. They have SelectNet, which is the internal electronic communication network (ECN) that serves to connect all market makers with one another and with the public. They also can trade on any other ECN, such as Instinet or the Island, where they can remain anonymous. Finally, they participate in the Small Order Execution System (SOES). These are the computer networks that serve to connect market makers and traders in the Nasdaq markets. Each of these systems functions with its own set of rules and characteristics. The rules constrain the actions of the market makers and, as a side effect, establish a pattern of trading for the market makers based on what kind of trade they are executing. Because market makers must follow these rules, and because we know what their functions are as employees of large Wall Street firms, by observing their actions in the marketplace, we can get an idea of their true trading intentions. Insofar as we can guess what the market makers' intentions are, we are able to enter or exit trades at opportune moments. By looking at where and how market makers trade on these systems, and by recognizing their trading strategies from the signals they send to the market, we can position ourselves successfully in the markets.

One may ask why there is so much focus on the existence and behavior of market makers in the Nasdaq. That is, who cares if there are market makers? As long as they are there to provide liquidity, all the better for us. This would, however, be an extremely simple and, some would argue, naive way of looking at the price movements of the Nasdaq. Beyond the fact that market makers are watching and trading actively in the markets all day, they are consciously moving and manipulating prices and momentum all day because their livelihood depends on it. The structure of the Nasdaq markets is such that no one knows exactly what the order flow is or how much stock is demanded or supplied at any given point in time. That is, since everyone is participating at home or in their trading terminals, one would have to read people's minds to have a picture of how much stock market participants are planning to buy or sell. One minute there may be very little interest in a stock, and then a big buyer may appear and start buying every share available. In this environment, market makers receive large orders to buy or sell stock for their institutional clients. It would be easier for them to coordinate large buy orders from one institutional client with large sell orders from another. In this way, they could earn their commissions and make their clients happy because they did not have to buy at a high price or sell at a low price. They could coordinate their high-volume buys with their high-volume sales and not move prices so much. This does not occur for many reasons. First of all, this would take place in an auction market, such as the New York Stock Exchange (NYSE). As we saw in previous chapters, this is the role of the specialist on the NYSE. As mentioned earlier, however, the Nasdaq markets are dealer-driven markets. The Nasdaq allows multiple dealers to compete against each other, so there are tighter spreads and more efficiency, rather than one specialist having knowledge of the current market demand. As far as the Nasdaq is concerned, if there were some way that someone knew all the order flow, this all-knowing individual would most likely exploit this information for himself or herself. This knowledge would amount to knowing the internal orders of all the major brokerage houses on Wall Street, as well as all other market participants. If we gave someone this knowledge, we might as well give him or her a license to mint money.

    As a result, we have a series of market makers who are all coming to the markets with their own orders and must attempt to buy at the lowest prices or sell at the highest prices possible, even though they have orders that could move prices significantly.[1] In this environment, market makers

---

[1] See the appendix to this chapter for a list of Nasdaq market makers.

must conceal their true intentions of buying or selling because if the other traders knew what they were, they would force the market maker to pay higher prices or sell at lower prices. Market makers have several ways of concealing their orders and of goading other market participants into handing over stocks at bargain prices.

The basic idea behind their strategies is to make other market participants believe that they should sell when the market maker has to buy; equivalently, they want to make the others believe that they should buy when the market maker has to sell. In so doing, however, they have to abide by two main rules, which are their Achilles' heel. The rules are

1   They cannot back away from the markets.
2   They must honor their quotes.

Recall that when we say that a market maker is backing away from the market, we say that he or she is setting a bid much lower than the highest bid and an offer much higher than the lowest bid. By not being near the inside market, the market maker will most likely not have to trade with other market participants. Backing away from the markets is taboo for market makers because they are not fulfilling the spirit of their roles as liquidity providers. The Wall Street community shuns this type of behavior. As a result, all the market makers have to stay near the inside market throughout the trading day. That is, their bid must be near or at the high bid or their offer must be near or at the low offer throughout the trading day. What this means for us is that they cannot be far from where we can see them. We do not need to keep an eye on every market maker in a stock at all times; however, when one of them is on the move, it is a good idea to see what they are doing and on which side of the inside market they appear. I will have more to say about this later.

The second rule means that market makers cannot costlessly misrepresent their intentions on the market. They cannot, for example, say that they are willing to buy at higher prices, in an effort to get the price to increase, because they will have to honor those higher prices to sellers. As a result, when market makers bid or offer, they are broadcasting signals about their trading intentions. While they may send out a signal completely contrary to their final trading objective, since it costs them to do so, they cannot fool the market for too long. We can think of this as a poker game. The market makers who bluff face the danger that a trader will call them on their bluff. If they bluff about higher prices, a trader may sell to them at these higher prices, and then they are stuck with that purchase.

These two rules together force market makers to remain visible throughout the markets and to represent themselves genuinely. In this way, we can see what they are doing. When we see them on our trading screens, whatever offers or bids they make are genuine and not just cheap talk. The one exception to this is when market makers are appearing on trading screens before the markets open. At this point, since trading cannot occur, they can offer or bid any amount and price they choose. The environment here is one in which no one knows the exact size or price at which the market will level off, and the uncertainty of the situation leads to a somewhat chaotic environment. Sometimes, for example, markets will be crossed, and bids will be higher than offers. But this is pure cheap talk. Market makers are simply feeling the market out and jockeying for position. They know that there is no credibility to their bids, so they use them as free advertising to one another and to the rest of the market. By the time the market does open, market makers have all corrected their bids and offers and are trading normally. At this point, they are all aware that they must honor their bids and offers on the market.

At the opening of the markets, trading is very hectic. The opening of the markets is like opening a floodgate of back orders that have accumulated throughout the night and early morning. People may have seen things on the news or have decided to buy or sell based on the closing price of a stock from the previous day. Whatever their motivation, many people call their brokers or place their own orders early at the market opening. The chaos and volatility of the trading early in the day present a great opportunity for market makers. They can fill large orders, and the markets are moving with such speed that the orders go unnoticed.

I recommend not trading during the morning rush. There is no clear picture of what is going on in the markets. When the market information and prices are moving so quickly and unpredictably, the market makers have enormous advantages. As was mentioned, they can hide amid all the chaos. They can push prices more easily and unload orders where it is best for them. Furthermore, since the markets are so volatile and unpredictable, the publicly available market information is not nearly as informative as the internal information that the market makers possess about their order flow. That is, in the openings, market participants cannot rely on what the price was 30 seconds ago to predict where the price is now because the markets are gyrating. Market makers, however, know their own internal order flow and can infer from it where the market price will be more or less. For example, if 9 of every 10 of their customers is frantically begging to sell XYZ stock, the market makers will have a pretty good idea of whether the price of the stock will fall or rise that day. We have no idea what anyone else is thinking, and the market positions slip away like soap in our hands. This is why market makers have such an advantage in the mornings, because they have their internal order flow as a leading indicator of market activity for that day and where the price will be. Whenever the price goes too high, they come in and sell like crazy, and when it is too low, they buy back their positions. Since in this battle we small investors do not have the elements to win, it is best to avert it altogether or be very careful in trading at the opening. Waiting a few minutes could save a lot of money.

After the opening, the market settles into its daily trading routine. Here, prices are usually much less unpredictable than at the opening, and we can more easily follow the market makers. The general idea of looking to what the market makers are doing is that since they are big fish, and we are the little fish, we can trade in the same direction as they trade and make money as they make money. In other words, we are hoping to catch the market makers as they begin to move a stock price in some direction and trade with the move. In essence, we are going to trade with the flow of the market. In order to do so, we must determine if the prices are increasing or decreasing. If we think that prices are increasing, we will take the long position, and vice versa if we think they are decreasing. The orders that will push prices up or down are most likely handled by market makers. As a result, we will look to see which market makers are actively pushing prices to determine which position to take.

Figure 7-1 lays out the possible areas where a stock price may be. The stock price is somewhere on the vertical line, which starts at zero and ends at some very large number. This means that the stock price can be at least zero, if it is worthless, and goes up from there. What we care about is the bid price and the offer price (or ask price). There are three regions marked A, B, and C in the figure. Region A encompasses the prices below the bid price, region B is the inside market, and region C is the area of prices above the offer price.

Generally speaking, when market makers quote two-way markets, they do one of the following: They quote on or very close to the bid and offer somewhere in region C, or they quote on or very close to the offer

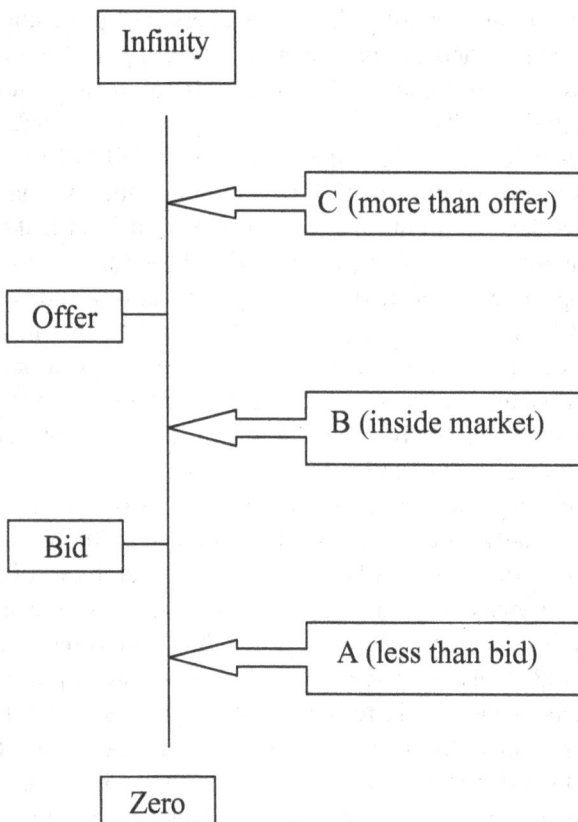

Figure 7-1. Possible areas for a stock price.

and bid somewhere in region *A*. Recall that region *B* is the inside market. How market makers move from one region to another reveals whether they are trying to push prices up or down and whether they are buyers or sellers on the market.

Starting from the Bid
We begin with a market maker who is on the bid. Suppose that this market maker has not been very active in the markets for most of the day, and you suspect that he or she is now filling a large order. The market maker's last quote was on the bid, but this was while the market maker was more or less inactive in the stock. Suppose that the market maker bought stock on the bid. Now the following options are available:

1 Move to *A*, i.e., lowers the bid.
2 Stay on the bid.
3 Move to *B*, i.e., raise the high bid, on the inside market.
4 Move to the offer.
5 Move to *C*, i.e., just above the offer.

Case 1: The market maker has bought and lowered his or her bid. In this case, the market maker is buying repeatedly, indicating a lack of interest in simply fulfilling the role as a provider of liquidity. A market maker interested in simply providing liquidity would buy some stock at the bid, move to the offer to unload it, and make the spread. This market maker is instead buying and bidding to buy again. The fact that the market maker is buying again implies a move toward the long position and the belief that the market is not in a hurry to increase prices. Ask yourself the following question: If you found a bargain at a flea market, would you haggle with the seller for a lower price, knowing that someone else could notice the bargain and take it out of your hands? Probably not, right? Well, this market maker is haggling with the market. The market maker bought, but is willing to buy again at a lower price, so he or she must not think that the stock is such a hot bargain that other buyers will swoop in and steal the bargain. The market maker may, for example, believe that the price will increase but that others are not aware of it yet, and that he or she can get a lower price from the market.

Case 2: The market maker has bought on the bid and stays on the bid. This market maker has bought at the going rate and continues to take long positions at the going rate. An analogy is the shopper who has found a bargain at a flea market and is taking as much of it as possible before others come and buy it all, thus preventing him or her from taking advantage of the low prices. This market maker is a buyer but does not believe it necessary, or even worthwhile, to push the price up. However, the market maker is not interested so much in getting a lower price as in getting the right quantity at the going price. Recall that the basic problem faced by market makers (as for all market participants) consists of trading off the risk of not getting the right price versus the risk of not getting the right quantity. If they try to bleed the market in terms of prices, they may not find enough sellers to take the opposite position. If they do not pay enough attention to prices, they will certainly find sellers at high prices but will lose money overpaying. In this case, the market maker is concerned with getting the quantity and is willing to pay the price going at the market.

Case 3: The market maker goes from the bid to a new, higher bid. This market maker is very bullish on the stock. He or she is aggressively taking the long position and basically stomping out other buyers. By raising the price, the market maker is expressing the willingness to buy a lot or at least would like people to believe this. A market maker who is repeatedly doing this is looking to buy, and the stock will go higher. This market maker is most likely buying for some customer. The main concern is to fill the order at the going prices which the market maker considers good enough to purchase at.

Another possible scenario for case 3 and, to some extent, for case 2 is that the market maker is interested in pushing up the price in the belief that many people are short on the stock. Believing this to be the case, the market maker may push up the price, knowing that the price can be pushed up high enough, it will be possible to squeeze these traders into buying to cover their shorts. Their buying will further accelerate the price increase. The market maker, who will be long on the stock, will reap the profits from the price increases that result from those traders who are trying to cover their shorts. In this case, the market maker may keep raising the bid and buying the offers. The market maker will buy on the bid and buy the stock on the offer and push up the price of both.

Case 4: The market maker buys on the bid and then moves to the offer. In this situation, the market maker made a purchase and then immediately attempted to sell stock back to the markets. A market maker uninterested in the stock would move just above the offer thus avoiding having to trade so much and can make a wider spread. In this case, the fact that the market maker is moving from one side of the inside market to the other indicates an attempt to hide the intention to buy or sell. A market maker who is buying more than he or she is selling is overall long on the stock and thinks that its value will increase.

Case 5: The market maker buys on the bid and offers to sell at a price just above the ask price. Here, if the amount offered is equal to the amount purchased on the bid, then the market maker most likely is uninterested in this stock possibly because of working a deal in another stock. The market maker is probably trying to provide liquidity and not back away from the market too much while at the same time not be tied up trading this stock.

Note, however, that we are assuming that the amount being offered is the same as the amount the market maker purchased on the bid. Sometimes market makers buy on the bid and then show a very large quantity for sale at a price above the offer, somewhere in region C. Then the market maker withdraws the big offer, hoping that people will believe that a huge sell-off is about to occur and will try to sell. Essentially, what the market maker is doing is advertising a large amount for sale and then withdrawing the advertisement before someone takes him or her up on it. The market maker is bluffing so that hopefully others believe that with such a great quantity about to enter the market, the price will fall, and they should sell while they can get high prices. If this occurs, then the market maker is most likely a buyer looking to shake out a few nervous investors and get a good price. A market maker who was really selling a large amount would not advertise it because that might cause a large price decline and force him or her to sell at lower prices.

Starting from the Offer

We begin with a market maker who is on the bid. Now we consider a market maker who has just sold stock on the offer. He or she then has one of the following options:

1   Move to C, i.e., raise the offer.
2   Stay on the offer.
3   Move to B, i.e., lower the low offer, on the inside market.
4   Move to the bid.
5   Move to A, i.e., just below the bid

Case 6: The market maker has sold stock and has moved to a lower offer. This case is analogous to case 1. Here, being a repeated seller, the market maker is taking the short position in the markets. Furthermore, the market maker will not even take the short position at the current price but rather will do so only at higher prices. Recall that this means that the market maker is confident of getting higher prices for buying or, equivalently, feels that at this point in time taking the short position should be compensated with a higher price. Although possibly haggling for higher selling prices at that moment, ultimately the market maker believes that the prices will fall. The market maker is bearish in what he or she believes is a bullish market. That is, the market maker is selling but is not willing to lower the price. The flea market example illustrates this position, just like in case 1. The market maker is willing to ask for a higher sale price, believing that there are buyers present willing to pay higher prices. The market maker believes that more could be gotten for the going sale price and is willing to try for higher prices, just like a vendor who sees that there are buyers willing to pay higher prices for goods at the flea market.

Case 7: The market maker has sold on the offer and stays on the offer. This market maker sold at the market price and is continuing to take short positions at the going rate. The market maker may be compared to a vendor who is unloading evergreens near the Christmas holidays at the local shopping mall parking lot. The vendor must get out while the getting is good and is not going to haggle too much before the merchandise really declines in value. The market maker faces the same prospect. The market maker is selling repeatedly at the going rate and concentrating on solidifying his or her short position, not on getting a high sale price. From the market maker's perspective, the benefits of this trade do not come now in the form of higher sale prices but rather later in the form of lower buying prices to cover shorts or to buy back the stock sold from inventory.

Case 8: The market maker goes from the offer to a new lower offer, i.e., region *B*. This case is analogous to case 3. Here, the market maker is very bearish on the stock. Not merely willing to sell and to sell at lower prices, the market maker is actually the one pushing the prices down. A market maker who repeatedly is the low offer is looking to sell and establish a short position quickly. The market maker likely is selling for a customer and needs the sale more than to maintain the current sale price. The market maker's customer most likely has been informed that the sale will occur at lower prices, and the customer has agreed, so long as the order is filled.

There is the extreme case of the market maker pushing the price down to cause investors who are long on the stock to panic and sell their positions. This is the same as the market maker who pushes prices up to catch investors with the short squeeze. Pushing prices down to get people to sell out their long positions, however, is not as effective as pushing prices up to get people to cover their shorts. The reason is that people are more likely to sit on their long positions and hope for a rebound, whereas the losses from shorting a rising stock manifest themselves more intensely and tend to affect markets more. A market maker who were to try this would have to keep lowering the offer and selling, as well as selling to the inside bids, and pushing prices down. If this can be continued until the market picks up the selling momentum, the market maker will be short on a falling market and stands to make a hefty profit. If the price refuses to fall, the market maker has sold a lot of stock at bargain prices.

Case 9: The market maker sells on the offer and then moves to the bid. After selling at the going rate, the market maker tries to buy back the stock. This case is analogous to case 4. Here, by working both sides of the inside market, the market maker most likely is concealing or delaying a price movement. The probable assumption is that there is no consensus at present in the market as to whether prices are rising or falling and the market maker does not want to set prices in motion against himself or herself. A market maker who is selling more than he or she is buying is probably selling off some extra stock from inventory. The market maker is overall selling more than he or she is buying, so, in any case, he or she is taking the short position and believes that prices are high at that moment.

Case 10: The market maker sells on the offer and then positions himself or herself just below the bid, somewhere in region *A*. This is analogous to the market maker not participating in case 5. If he or she is selling and buying similar amounts, then this market maker is providing liquidity and is not actively taking positions in this stock. The individual is simply making markets and trying to not have to trade too much while at the same time not backing away from the markets. Furthermore, this is all under the assumption that the market maker is buying and selling similar quantities. If not, i.e., if the market maker suddenly shows an enormous quantity at a bid just below the current bid, he or she may be trying to scare people who are short on the stock into buying. This could work if people buy into the idea that a bid quantity is going to be demanded soon; however, they would have to believe that a big buyer would advertise it at a bid lower than the current bid. This would, if it were true, move against the best interest of the supposed buyer, so it is not credible. All the same, some investors cover their shorts when this type of maneuver is done. The market maker runs the risk of some large seller being present in the markets at that very instant and forcing him or her to buy the large amount, instead of the seller having to move the price lower to unload the large order.

From Either the Bid or the Offer

The last scenario occurs infrequently.

Case 11: This is the unusual case in which the market maker bids above the offer or offers below the bid. That is, the market maker offers in region *A* or bids in region *C*. This is very rare and does not last long because it gives any investor the instantaneous possibility to buy and resell for a profit. When this occurs, the market maker is telling the market in no uncertain terms that he or she is ready to move prices. One possibility for this is that the market maker simply has a large order to fill. Another possibility is that the market maker is trying to cause a surge in prices or get them to fall precipitously in order to buy or sell at very good prices due to a buying or selling frenzy.

MARKET MAKERS ON ECNs

The preceding scenarios are detectable only insofar as the market makers' movements are detectable. We can see what market makers are doing on SelectNet, so this is the vehicle for observing them. They know that they are being observed when they trade on SelectNet, so they are aware that their actions are being broadcast to the entire trading community. Furthermore, they know that we know that they are being watched, and we know that they know that we know that they are being watched, and they know that we know. . . . The point is that the other ECNs do not broadcast what the market makers are doing and maintain their anonymity. As a result, market makers have the ability to complement their trading on SelectNet, which is where they advertise their intentions, with their trading on other ECNs, which is where they may carry out anonymous trades. Prices on all the ECNs are never too different for too long because that would create arbitrage opportunities. As a result, the market makers can try to counteract the pressure of their buying on some ECN with the appearance of selling on SelectNet. This, of course, has a limited effect because of the fact that stock prices on all the electronic markets move parallel to one another. If a market maker can succeed in countering the pressures of buying for just a few moments on one ECN by offering inside the market on SelectNet, it may be enough to fill his or her trade. The market maker just needs to sustain the low price while completing the trade and establishing the beneficial position. Then, when backing away from the offer and moving to the bid, the market maker is long on the stock, and the price shoots up. In these types of maneuvers, the market makers are exploiting the fact that the supply and demand of stock are disaggregated in the Nasdaq markets among the ECNs, whereas the price at which any given stock trades is the same. They pretend to sell but are in reality buying from ECNs more than they are selling. If their order flow were consolidated, they would not be able to pull this off, but since no one knows who is buying, they can do it sometimes.

INSTITUTIONAL MARKET PARTICIPANTS

Institutional market participants are the big buyers of stock on the market, such as pension funds, mutual funds, insurance companies, and others. They are similar to small investors in that they may look to invest in stocks, unlike market makers, who make money from commissions and spreads, beyond the income they generate from trading on their inventory. In this sense, both institutional investors and small investors are subject to the rise and fall of the markets and must earn their profits from them. This is where the similarities end, however.

First of all, institutional investors have an immense war chest with which they trade. The volume that they trade generates for them a privileged status among the professional traders on Wall Street, as we saw with the market makers. Beyond the outstanding trading service they get in the markets, they have the ability to weather difficult trades beyond anything most small investors could do. For example, they have the capital to buy large tracts of stock and are not fazed by small movements in prices, where a day trader would sell out a much smaller-sized lot at the first moderate downturn. On the other hand, having too much money when the markets are saturated can lead to bad investments, but they are forced to participate in the markets as people invest in them. They can afford very competent staff to analyze the markets and do sophisticated modeling and research. Their networks of employees keep in close contact with others in the financial world and with the rumors of Wall Street, and as a result, the managers of these institutions often know what is going on before the financial press does.

Generally speaking, these organizations are simply another source of pressure on the markets. They all are more or less trying to beat the S&P500, which is not so easy considering how many millions of dollars they invest. Their job is to keep their investors happy, which translates into not looking bad relative to the other institutions that are investing in the markets. Mutual fund managers, for example, have to deal with the ratings in financial magazines. The manager of the lowest-return fund does not look good. The impact of mutual fund managers on small investors, however, is not direct, like the impact of market makers. While they move stock prices, their goal is to trade against the market as a whole, not against any one group of traders in particular. As was mentioned in Chapter 6, the managers of these institutions sometimes give expert opinions that are obviously skewed to benefit their portfolios. Additionally, mutual fund managers may load up on hot or popular stocks toward the end of the year so that they show up on their fund's prospectus. All these institutional investors make big waves in the market because of their size. They cannot help but be noticed when they buy or sell because they buy or sell tons of shares every time. This hurts them tremendously if they get into trouble because getting out of a bad stock without sustaining heavy losses can be very difficult. As a result, at the first sign of trouble, they stampede to the blue chips and to other safe havens. Since they are so big, any time they abandon a group of stocks, there is a massive sell-off. They may believe that there is a massive sell-off looming and escape to more stable stocks. However, this drop in prices is caused and each time reinforced by their very leaving. It is a self-fulfilling prophecy for big institutions to think that they should dump a stock because its price will fall. Of course a company's stock price will fall if a big institution dumps its stock. When these flights to quality occur in the markets, look out, because if you are not in blue chips, everything else may hit rock bottom.

SMALL INVESTORS

Small investors refers to us. As we have seen in previous chapters, there are many different kinds of small investors. One way to capture these differences is to examine how each kind of small investor looks at stock prices. An example helps illustrate how different investors look at the behavior of stock prices. A stock price is fluctuating up and down throughout the day, but over time it follows a trend. Some people have compared this phenomenon with that of a person walking a dog. If we look at the movement of the dog, we see that it goes back and forth, seeming almost random. If we step back, however, we can see that the dog is only running around the person, who may be walking the dog around the block, for example. When investors are trading in the very short run, they are trying to guess what the movement of the dog will be from moment to moment. When investors are taking long-run positions, they are more concerned with anticipating which way the owner will walk and what is motivating him or her to take one path or another.

These small investors will adopt trading strategies according to the market signals they receive, the signals that we have described thus far. They trade with strong groups and strong stocks. Stocks that are falling may rebound, but there may be quite a while before that occurs. Instead, trade long on strong stocks and short on weak ones. Always go with the flow. Trade on the coattails of the market giants. We have seen how prices move and the influence of market giants on prices. There is no reason to try to buck the trend; there is plenty of money to be made by trading behind the big influences that move the markets. Trading against them only gets the small investor swept aside and is a sure way to lose money.

Some investors use statistics based on company fundamentals such as price-earnings (P/E) ratios, book value versus market value, debt ratios, growth indicators, market share indicators, stock splits, and others to decide which stocks to buy. Other investors use charting techniques or look at intraday market dynamics to try to pick stocks. No wise investor picks stocks impulsively or on a hunch. This is not the way to make money. Always have a good reason for taking a position in a stock.

When entering a trade, small investors realize that even on an ECN it is difficult and rare to make the spread on trades. Small investors trade by buying on the offer and selling on higher offers or on the bid if need be. Also, one should keep an eye on the average number of levels that the stock moves. In order to get the best prices, it is important to be aware of where the stock price is in relation to its support and its resistance. Since the stock moves about the same number of levels on each run, we can enter close to a momentum swing. One should be aware of from whom one is buying when buying on an ECN. If a small investor buys from a market maker on an ECN and that market maker is also selling on SelectNet, for example, it is a good idea to get out of that trade fast, because the market maker is unloading. This is especially true if the market maker is pushing the stock price down. On the other hand, if listed as a bidder, the market maker may be reselling some stock that he or she had to buy because of SOES.

SOES is the best friend of the small investor. This system will serve as the parachute for bad trades and hectic market situations. In the beginning, a prudent strategy is to trade blocks under 1000 shares so that a SOES escape from any position is only a click away for the small investor. This minimizes the losses of a trade, losses that will be incurred naturally by anyone trading in the markets. The key to being able to sustain these losses and continue to trade and make money is to manage them. No loss should ever be so big that it wipes out the capital with which the small investor trades.

Small investors realize that they participate in the markets and can be shaken by the maneuvers of the market makers. This is going to happen occasionally, but one should not fall prey to these types of maneuvers on a regular basis. If, for example, prices are increasing and then they stop, one should not try to sell immediately. This only helps swing the momentum in the opposite direction. Instead, the small investor should back off and give the market a chance to catch its breath and keep on climbing. In cases where the stock could go higher, if you sell, you sold out too soon. In cases where the stock will not go higher, if you try to sell on the offer, you are only ushering in the decline of the stock price faster. By waiting, you could capture the benefits of the price increases, and in cases where the price declines, in all likelihood you would have to sell on the bid, not the offer.

Note that if other traders panic and rush to get their stock on the offer, they may start the sell-off, and the price decline, so you should be ready to hit the bid, not try to sell on the offer. Also, the trader can guard against this by using limit orders. These provide an automatic exit to bad trades and can be very useful for the small investor.

This chapter has dealt with the general categories of market participants. While Chapter 6 described the information used to steer the herd of traders, this chapter looked at who is in the herd, who leads, and who follows. We saw the role of market makers and their three functions in the market. They are to make markets, fill their clients' orders, and take positions of their own. We also saw the elusive trading strategies market makers employ when they wish to trade without moving prices against themselves. Finally, the rules by which market makers must abide constrain them to certain patterns of trading, which we can use to detect which way pressure is brought to bear on prices. We also looked at institutional clients and retail clients and some of their trading behavioral patterns. The next chapter looks at some ways to get involved in the markets.

QUESTIONS

1   How much should a trader or small investor rely on SOES for liquidating his or her positions, and how far can such investors stray from the 1000-share limit, where SOES can no longer bail them out?

2   With so many ECNs and market makers, is it difficult to detect when one of them in particular is making a large buy for a client, for example?

3   What sort of speculative positions do market makers take that can benefit or hurt the small investor?

4   Is it possible for a market maker to corner a stock? Explain what "cornering a stock" means.

5   How much of an advantage do market makers have from knowing their own internal order flow beyond the market information?

APPENDIX: MARKET MAKERS

There are over 500 firms making markets on the Nasdaq. On average, for example, there are 11 firms making markets per security. For some high-visibility stocks, there can be as many as 60 firms making markets. Below is a list of some of the most prominent market makers. Note, however, that this list is not exhaustive.

Arnhold & Bleichroeder	ABLE	Dain, Bosworth	DAIN
Alex, Brown & Sons	ABSB	Dean Witter Reynolds	DEAN
A. G. Edwards & Sons	AGED	Donaldson, Lufkin & Jenrette	DLJP
J. Alexander Securities	ALEX	Dillon, Read	DRCO
Fred Alger & Co.	ALGR	Ernst & Co.	ERNS
Robert W. Baird & Co.	BARD	Everen Securities	EVRN
Bear, Stearns	BEST	First Albany Corp.	FACT
Bt Securities	BTSC	Fahnestock & Co.	FAHN
Cantor, Fitzgerald & Co.	CANT	Credit Suisse First Boston	FBCO
ABM Amro Chicago	CHGO	Gruntal & Co.	GRUN
Coastal Securities	COST	Goldman Sachs	GSCO
Cowen & Co.	COWN	GVR Co.	GVRC

Hambrecht & Quist	HMQT	Knight Securities	NITE
Herzog, Heine, Geduld	HRZG	Nomura Securities	NMRA
J. B. Oxford	JBOC	Olde Discount Corp.	OLDE
Jefferies & Co.	JEFF	Oppenheimer & Co.	OPCO
J. P. Morgan Securities	JPMS	Prudential Securities	PRUS
John G. Kinnard & Co.	KINN	Punk Ziegel & Knoell	PUNK
Kidder Peabody	KPCO	PaineWebber	PWJC
Legg Mason Wood Walker	LEGG	Ragen McKenzie	RAGN
Lehman Brothers	LEHM	Raymond, James & Associates	RAJA
Bernard L. Madoff	MADF	Rauscher Pierce Refsnes	RPSC
Schwab	MASH	Salomon Brothers	SALB
M. H. Meyerson & Co.	MHMY	SBC Warburg	SBCW
Merril Lynch	MLCO	Sands Brothers & Co.	SBNY
Montgomery Securities	MONT	Smith Barney	SBSH
Morgan Stanley	MSCO	Sherwood Securities	SHWD
Chicago Stock Exchange	MSWE	Tucker Anthony	TUCK
Quick & Reilley	NAWE	Waterhouse Securities	WATH
Neddham & Co.	NEED	Wall Street Equities	WSEI

8

READY TO GO

In previous chapters we have looked at the workings of the stock markets, the role of different market participants, and the different approaches to investing available to the small investor. As diverse individuals come to the markets to invest their savings, we have seen the variety of instruments and approaches to investing that the capital markets permit. We have looked at the new options available to small investors and have seen that investing today can mean a variety of things to the many and varied market participants. The approach any one person takes toward investing can be as individual as the person is. Understanding the markets and understanding direct access trading in them become valuable only insofar as people with money to invest realize their potential gains. That is, investors must take the plunge into the new opportunities in order to realize the gains implied by the opportunities that the markets afford them. As a result, this chapter deals

with making the first steps in direct access trading. We will look at
examples of how to get involved in the markets and how to take advan-
tage of these new opportunities.

It probably comes as no surprise that at the most basic level, the first
step in direct access trading is equipping oneself with a computer. Direct
access trading is rooted in Internet technology and networking of markets,
so it is evident that a computer is necessary. A discussion of which systems are advisable is beyond the scope of this chapter. Given the simi-
larity and effectiveness of modern computers, it would be an unnecessary
and tedious digression. The important point is that trading depends on
becoming comfortable with the most basic workings of computers and
how to operate a windows environment and an Internet browser environment. For investors looking to day trade, a computer will serve, but leas-
ing a trading terminal at a trading firm also can be a substitute. The benefit
of a trading terminal is that the investor is in an environment of day
traders and can learn a lot from fellow traders.

After acquiring the necessary hardware, i.e., the computer for trading,
the next step is to get connected to the Internet. The importance of the
speed and reliability of the Internet connection will depend on the goal
and style of the individual investor. For a day trader, for example, reliability and speed are key for successful trading. The day trader trading
from home, for example, should consider having a separate telephone line
and a very reliable Internet service provider (ISP). If not, the trader may
be disconnected in the middle of the trading day, with positions open,
and lose a lot of money as prices shift. It is recommended that for extensive trading, such as day trading, one consider investing in a cable
modem and cable connection or a digital subscriber line (DSL). These
are Internet connections that are very fast and very reliable. For a long-
term investor, connecting is almost never the main concern. In this case,
the horizon of investing is such that a price movement of ⅛, for example,
will not be that devastating. Furthermore, the long-term investor can wait
out the intraday movements in prices.

Having the Internet connection established, the small investor is ready
to begin trading with direct access. As we have seen, this means that the
investor can circumvent the traditional media of investing, such as retail
stockbrokers, and use the computer to invest. One way of doing this is
to engage an online brokerage firm. Many people are currently using these
firms to invest. They are simple to use, and there are dozens and dozens

of companies offering this service. This book does not endorse any one online brokerage in particular. Given the competitive environment of the Internet, online brokerage firms tend to offer very similar services. That is, since a small investor using an online broker is always just a click away from that online broker's competitor, the competition among these firms is intense. Because of the ease of switching from one online broker to another, they are forced to price similarly and offer similar services.

An example of an online broker would be E*TRADE. This company runs a very popular online trading Web site; however, as mentioned earlier, E*TRADE competes with many other Web sites that provide very similar levels of services. E*TRADE Web pages generally serve to suggest stocks for investors to buy into. That is, the online brokerage firm puts together a Web page with some research and consolidates some market information so as to help the small investor select which stocks to buy. The small investor can look through the links on the Web page for articles on market performance, the performance of specific sectors in the market, or the performance of portfolios. When looking at stocks, these Web sites often offer historical data and charts describing the stock's performance over time. Also offered are articles appearing in the financial press regarding the stocks of interest to small investors. These articles chronologically document the market sentiment in relation to the stock and the important events that have occurred regarding the stock of interest, such as announcements of earnings, stock splits, mergers, and so on.

The service such Web pages provide includes level I quotes for investors. An investor interested in a stock may type in the stock symbol and receive the market quote for that stock. Other information will be included besides price and size, such as the day's high and low or the opening price and the change in the current price with respect to the opening price.

Beyond the basic price information, these Web pages show some portfolio selections and suggestions for investing. Recalling the definition of value stocks, the "Fair Value Portfolio," for example, is a portfolio of value stock suggestions. There are many Web sites that look at a company's fundamentals, such as its price to earnings ratios, and try to guess which stocks will appreciate. The "Platinum Portfolio" does more of the same type of value stock suggestion. Other categories, such as "Small Cap/IPO Portfolio" and "High Yield Portfolio," address some of the other type of investment goals presented earlier. The "Small Cap/IPO Portfolio," for example, could be viewed as the higher-risk, higher-growth portfolio suggestion, whereas the "High Yield Portfolio" is the suggestion this Web site makes for investors looking for income stocks. The "Power Pick Portfolio" is, as discussed in previous chapters, the portfolio that analysts are publicly endorsing. The implications of the public endorsement have already been discussed, and here we see the analysts' influence at work in the shaping of market opinion.

The opposing column of the Web page presents the small investor with choices of suggestions and articles about stocks and sectors of the market. A column labeled "Investment Insights" attempts to consolidate selected sectors and topics about the market. That is, the column brings certain sectors of the market to the forefront and highlights certain changes or events in the market. An example is that the Web page provides analyst upgrades and downgrades in the "Recent S&P Upgrades/ Downgrades" link. We have seen how an upgrade or downgrade can affect a stock, and this link serves to alert investors of changes in expectations. As a result, the link serves to alert investors to possible changes in the buying strategies or market sentiment of Wall Street. Another example of bringing selected information to the forefront is the selected stocks represented in the column, namely, GE and Cytyc Corp., or for selected sectors, in this case, the technology sector. The publicity generated for these stocks or sectors could lead to increased volume in trading of these stocks and hence price shifts. Finally, the Web page may have a link called "What's Hot/What's Not," which goes by many other names, depending on the Web site. This information is usually included because it lists the biggest movers in the market for that day or week. The biggest movers are the stocks with the largest price increases or declines. Recall that when a stock has a large movement, it draws attention to itself, which can lead to more movement. Furthermore, a large movement in a stock price could reverberate across other stocks in its sector, as we have seen. For this reason, it is important to keep an eye on this information.

Online brokerage firms generally show information on stocks in a similar fashion. The important point to remember is the feel for online investing that these types of firms give the small investor. First off, the online brokerage firms benefit from having a large order flow, and greater commissions, so it is to their benefit that the small investor trade more often. As a result, they try to make their Web pages as informative and user friendly as possible. These Web pages are designed to be educational and functional. They offer many services for the investor to learn to use them, and learn to invest in the market. While the responsibility to education in the financial markets is still our own, the Web pages will attempt to make the application of the information about how to invest as easy as possible for the small investor. It is useful, for example, to get on the computer and try out several Web pages, and find one that is most appealing and easy. Many Web pages encourage this by offering new-comers free trades at the beginning, or for a limited period of time. The important idea here is that one should be able to handle the Web page with ease, and should experiment and know how trades are conducted on these Web pages before committing money to the markets through them. It is also important to be aware of the fee structure of Web pages; for example, limit orders are usually more expensive than market orders. Additionally, investors that make a certain number of trades per month, for example, often can get a sort of volume discount on the commissions per trade. All this information is usually readily available on the Web pages of these kinds of online brokers, and it is in their interest to make the small investor both aware of the information, and feel comfortable using the Web page.

Online brokerage firms, however, are not usually in the business of providing Nasdaq level II quotes to small investors. Very recently, some large online brokerages have begun to incorporate themselves into this type of direct access to the markets. Usually, however, it is day trading firms that are expanding their business to new small investors that attract those looking for Nasdaq level II data. Recall that this information is the best description available of trading on the Nasdaq markets. It includes the names of market makers bidding on a stock and the volume of the stock, as well as many other kinds of information, and of course, all in real time.

Figure 8-1 is an example of a level II data screen from Trades-cape.com. Again, this book is not endorsing this provider, nor is this book dissuading the reader from using Tradescape.com. The figure shows the Nasdaq level II data screen for a given stock. We know that it is this stock because of the symbol MSFT in the box in the upper left-hand corner. Immediately following, we see what someone with "real time" quotes in an online brokerage firm usually sees. That is, the person gets Nasdaq level I data, which includes a quote of the best market available for the stock at every moment in time. The level I data include the highest bid and the quantity bid for (i.e., size of the bid), the lowest offer and

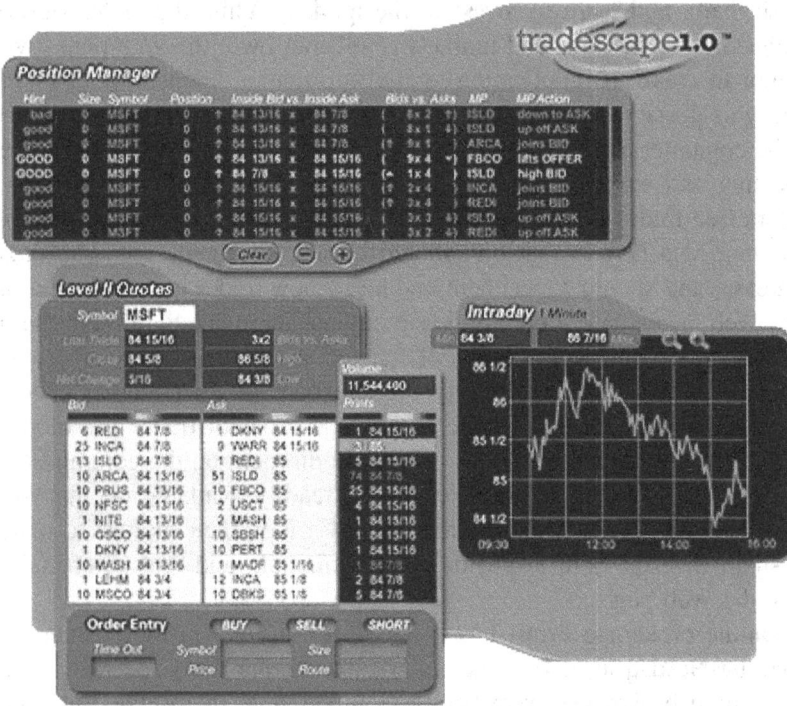

Figure 8-1. Nasdaq level II screen for a given stock. (*Courtesy of Tradescape.*)

the quantity offered (i.e., size of the offer), as well as the volume. The
advantage of level II data comes in the expanded information in the bottom screen.

We can look at the bid, for example. The list of bidders is sectioned
into different shades. Each shade represents a certain distance from the
high bid. The choice of shadings is up to the individual investor and is
only used as an aid for quickly summarizing the buying and selling pressure on any particular stock. It is not even necessary to have the shadings,
but many traders find them useful. For example, there are four market
participants on the inside bid, whereas there is only one on the inside
offer.

The level II window shows the inside market as it is developing. We
can see, for example, who is bidding. In this case, it is INCA, REDI,
RSSF, and MLCO, which are the symbols for Instinet (or Reuters), Re-
dibook (or Speer, Leeds, & Kellogg), Robertson Stephens & Co., and

Merrill Lynch & Co. This information is useful for knowing if a market maker is pushing a stock price up, if there is a big order on the market, and so on. This window represents the entire market for a stock, as can be best described for the Nasdaq market. The four columns describe the market maker's identification, the bid or offer price, the bid or offer size, and the time the bid was placed. The information in these four columns is the best snapshot available for the Nasdaq markets. This is why level II data are so useful.

The trading of stocks with level II quotes occurs on trading screens such as the one pictured in Figure 8-1. That is, the screen describes the market for one particular stock, in this case MSFT. Traders can keep track of the spot market for MSFT throughout the day with this type of screen. They look to the level II data to get a snapshot of the market activity for any one stock in which they are interested. Often they may have multiple screens like the one in the figure appearing at once as a part of a bigger screen used to manage their entire trading activity. Several types of trading screens are given in Figures 8-2 through 8-5.

Figure 8-4 shows one screen that Tradescape.com offers to its subscribers. Traders use this type of screen for high-frequency trading, such as day trading, swing trading, scalping, or intensely maintaining a very large portfolio. This screen offers connections to ECNs, as well as "smart" technology, to find the best prices across ECNs when filling a trade. Let's look at some of the features of this type of screen. At the very top are the indicators for the market as a whole, such as the Nasdaq Composite Index, the Dow Jones Industrial Average (DJIA), or the Standard & Poors 500 (S&P500). If these market-wide indicators are up on the day, they appear in green; if they are down, they appear in red. Generally, if a number or symbol appears in green, it is bullish, and if it appears in red, it is bearish.

The part of the screen labeled "Position Manager" (see Figure 8-5) keeps track of the market participants as they enter the market. This feature works to provide information on how market makers and other market participants move into and out of stocks. It turns the focus of the investor away from just prices and toward seeing how individuals involved in the market for a stock are manipulating the price. The level II quote screen appears in the bottom left-hand corner of the trading screen. It is the same as the level II screen in Figure 8-1, only smaller, to allow other things to fit in the screen. The portfolio tracking system is used to keep track of the money in the account of the small investor. Other sta-

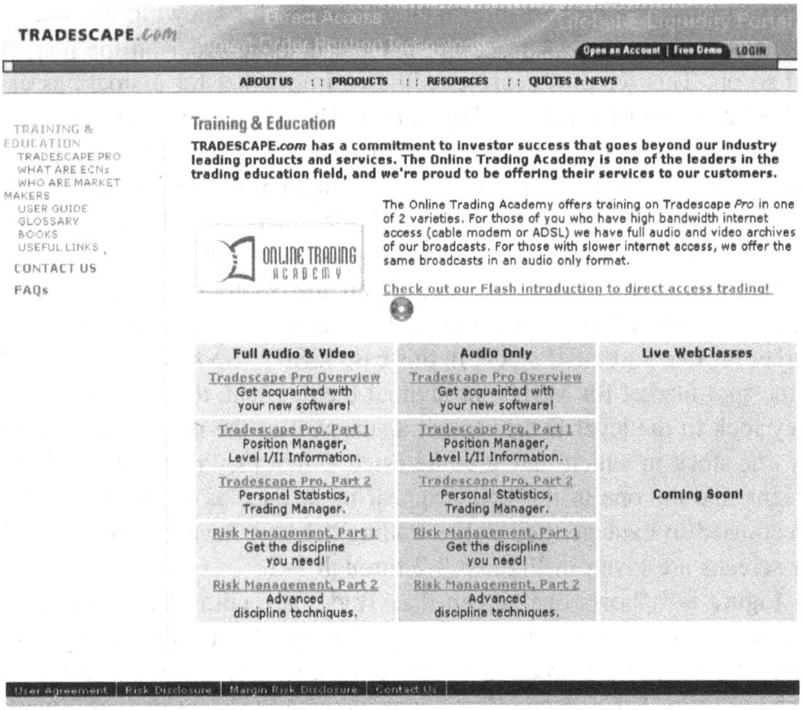

Figure 8-2. Tradescape.com training and education. (*Courtesy of Tradescape.*)

tistics describing profits and losses and the investor's open positions are also detailed. These are very important features because the trader must manage his or her capital in order to survive in the markets. Further features included in these kinds of trading screens are charts and graphs for the movement of stock prices. These are useful for looking at the past behavior of stock prices to gauge market sentiment for that stock. Chartists and technical analysts make extensive use of these kinds of charts.

Another important feature of these kinds of trading screens is that they offer simulators for investors to learn to trade and get a feel for the market without having to risk money (see Figure 8-3). These simulators work like a real trading screen and allow the beginning trader practice at running a trading screen and learning the basics of trading. They can be very useful for learning, because without practicing, small mistakes can be costly. Through training on a simulator, a trader can learn to manage an account and follow a stock and practice when to get in and out of

Direct Access

Global Liquidity Portal

Smart Order Routing Technology

Open an Account | Free Demo | LOGIN

ABOUT US : : **PRODUCTS** : : **RESOURCES** : : **QUOTES & NEWS**

ONLINE TRADING
FEATURES
PRICING
GETTING STARTED
USER GUIDE
FREE SIMULATOR
WHAT'S NEW

PROFESSIONAL
FEATURES

LEVEL II QUOTES
FEATURES
PRICING
GETTING STARTED

Free Simulator

Tradescape Challenge is a powerful simulation of our online trading technology. It's easy to use, and there's no risk involved. Whether you've traded before or you're just getting started, this is your chance to experience all the features that Tradescape PRO* has to offer:

- Level II Quotes (delayed 15 minutes)- dynamic market maker and ECN movements

- Smart Order Routing Technology™ - scans the market for the best possible price

- Electronic Communication Portal™ technology - connectivity to the top market makers and ECNs in each stock.

- Dynamic market indicators - measures of strength and volatility

- Fast Executions

▶ SIGN UP FOR TRADESCAPE CHALLENGE

*The actual trading platform has some additional features, but this game will allow you to sample our product and get a feel for trading with Tradescape.com.

User Agreement | Risk Disclosure | Margin Risk Disclosure | Contact Us

Figure 8-3. Tradescape.com free simulator. (*Courtesy of Tradescape.*)

Global Security Portal

Open an Account | Free Demo | LOGIN

Direct Access

ABOUT US :: **PRODUCTS** :: **RESOURCES** :: **QUOTES & NEWS**

ONLINE TRADING
FEATURES
PRICING
GETTING STARTED
USER GUIDE
FREE SIMULATOR
WHAT'S NEW
PROFESSIONAL
FEATURES

LEVEL II QUOTES
FEATURES
PRICING
GETTING STARTED

Professional Trading

Soon to be released online:

Lightspeed is the next generation of our FirstLevel™ trading software that is used by thousands of professional on-site traders. This stand-alone trading platform will allow remote customers to experience the superior software functionality and performance exclusively available to our on-site trading veterans.

To learn more about Lightspeed and when it will be available online please contact us at: Lightspeed@tradescape.com

See Lightspeed in action

Learn more about Lightspeed's features

- **Direct Connections to ECNs and Nasdaq**: Gain a competitive edge with faster information and faster trades.

- **Smart Order Routing**: Seek the best venue for executing your trade.

- **Customization and Filter Consoles**: Choose the data you want, the way you want to see it.

- **Thermographs**: Track the direction and intensity of market movements.

- **ECP Book**: View the best bids and offers from every ECN, centralized in a single book.

- **Latency Console**: Know the speed of each ECN before you trade.

User Agreement | Risk Disclosure | Margin Risk Disclosure | Contact Us

Figure 8-4. Tradescape.com market snapshot. (*Courtesy of Tradescape.*)

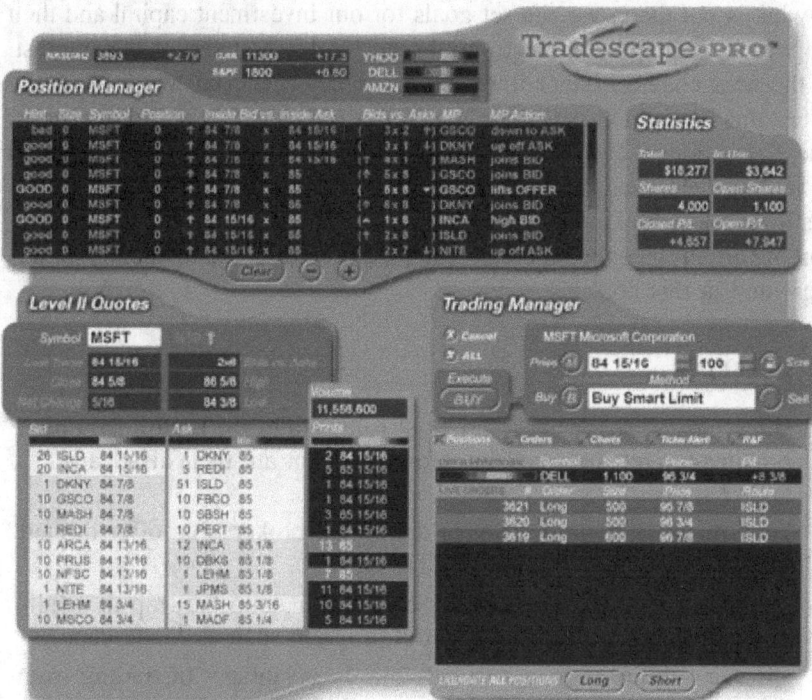

Figure 8-5. Tradescape.com "Pro Position Manager." (*Courtesy of Tradescape.*)

trades. Note, however, that these products are forgiving because mistakes on them do not cost the investor money, and thus they can lead to an investor learning to trade with excessive risk. That is, if the investor does not experience the full cost of a mistake when learning, he or she may not consider the mistake as grave. As a result, the investor may learn to trade with the false impression that mistakes are not as costly as they truly are and may take excessive risks as a result. For this reason, it is important to remember that a simulator is just like the real thing. When a trader loses money on one, it is not to be taken lightly, because it represents the possibility of losing real money on the markets. Figure 8-5 is the screen that Tradescape.com uses for its professional traders. It can handle a lot more information but functionally does the same thing.

In this chapter, we have seen the alternatives for getting online and trading in the markets. The best way to see what is on the Web, however, is to get online and investigate the alternatives for oneself. With an idea

of what is out there, we can set goals for our investment capital and then
see which Web site and electronic broker/dealer best serves our interest.
In the next chapter, rather than add more new material, we look at the
issues this book addresses through a series of frequently asked questions.
These questions were posed to some colleagues working at the vanguard
of trading technology. Their opinions on some of the issues relevant to
small investors looking to enter the market are presented, with the intention of further widening and clarifying the picture of the financial markets
presented in this book.

QUESTIONS

1   What are the advantages and what role should the traditional online
    broker play for the small investor, and what are their disadvan-
    tages?

2   How much of an improvement are online brokers that offer limited
    level II data, such as Power E*TRADE?

3   When should the small investor consider making the leap to a full-
    fledged level II workstation with a program such as Tradescape?

4   What are the relative advantages and disadvantages of trading from
    home versus a trading firm?

5   What are some of the best ways to stay current on the development
    of applications of trading technology that could benefit the small
    investor? What developments could possibly further change the
    trading landscape for small investors?

9

QUESTIONS AND ANSWERS

When one wants to reduce the risk of an investment, one diversifies one's portfolio so as to reduce the variance of the return. That is, by spreading one's money over many assets, one reduces the chances of losing money, because while one of the assets may lose money, it is improbable that they all will lose money. This is the age-old idea of not putting all one's eggs in a single basket. The concept of diversifying one's investment to reduce the uncertainty of the return is not confined to the stock market, however.

One can view reading a book as an investment, where one invests time in learning about a topic. Accordingly, in order to better diversify the ideas presented in this book about the markets, this chapter includes a series of opinions on trading and investing by some friends and colleagues involved in direct access trading. By including their opinions on some frequently asked questions, the chapter serves to diversify the informational content and opinions on investing so as not to put all the reader's eggs in one basket either.

A caveat to including these opinions is that they are exactly that—opinions. They are included for the aforementioned purposes, and in keeping with not misrepresenting the individuals who were kind enough to contribute these opinions, they have been edited as little as possible and only for the purposes of making the text more understandable. That is, as much as possible, their content reflects only the views of those interviewed and not necessarily the opinion of the author of this book.

INTERVIEW ONE

Q: Talking about people with a small amount of investment capital to start, what are the realistic expectations for a beginner who is just starting out?

A: A common beginner's expectation is that he or she will not lose any money. But beginners must realize that it is a losing proposition, even for experienced traders. If a person can get in there and learn and not lose money, that's fantastic. I've seen a lot of beginners come in and lose money, and that's expected, but that's just something that we tell everyone that comes into the business, probably the first few months you're going to lose money. So if you can get by without losing any money, that's a huge, huge bonus. I think that after about 6 months of trading and learning, the investor probably can expect to start making a good return on his or her money.

Q: It has to be hard, especially when you're starting and you're going up against professionals who are doing it day in and day out and have been in the markets for a while. What are some of the safer strategies you can use when you're just starting out?

A: When I've trained people, I've always suggested they play nonvolatile stocks with tight spreads, and a stock that has a lot of liquidity. Obviously, that's the name of the game in training, managing liquidity. So if the beginner can see what the liquidity is, know how to get in and out of stocks, I think he or she is going to learn a lot and not lose any money. There are other traders who have a different philosophy, where they try to train people, try to get them to play the spreads that are like two points wide. Buy 100 shares, try to make the spread. Boom, you make $200. That's a very dangerous way to teach someone who's completely new to the industry. Start beginners off on a stock that's under $50, and there's a lot of [liquidity] that trades by quarters rather than points. I think you can learn just dynamics, market maker dynamics, instead of just intraday, day trading noise. That's probably the most basic. I just try to tell beginners, "That's how I was taught, to play less volatile stocks with a lot of liquidity. You don't get a lot of bang for your buck but you're not going to lose all your money in the first few months."

Q: Is it better to start off kind of watching a smaller group of stocks than trying to really go in a lot of different directions at once?

A: I think it depends on the person. The way I was taught, I was taught on just watching a handful of stocks every day. I avoided the Internets in the beginning. Now the Internet stocks are dead, so somebody could watch the Internet sector. But when I first started off in the sector, Internets were crazy, so my trainer told me to not look at the Internets. I also suggest that, unless you want to play them, because that's where the volatility is, that's where a lot of so-called easy money is. But I only started playing them when I felt comfortable with more kinds of trading, like swing trading and day trading.

I think in the beginning it's good to watch a handful of stocks, but as you get more experienced, you definitely want to be able to play all sorts of stocks. You may want to play the small caps, the big caps, the $2 stocks, the $300 stocks. If you can learn on everything, you'll really have longevity in this business.

In the beginning I used to be so pigeonholed in terms of the types of stocks I played. I started expanding, and I'm still learning how to play different stocks. In a crazy market like this, you have to adjust your style on the fly.

Q: Staying with the topic of starting, let's say somebody is starting with a small amount of investment capital. How much money can the beginner realistically hope to begin making or hope to avoid losing in a single day? Can investors kind of hedge their bets? Is it still possible to make it in the business starting with a small amount of investment capital?

A: I don't know what small is, maybe less than $25,000? I think it's tough. I've only seen a handful of people—actually a couple of guys I work with, they just started with $25,000. They've already quadrupled their money in less than 3 months. That's because . . .

Q: They've had some good training.

A: Yeah, good training is essential. The more you learn, the better, and the more good people around you, the better still. If the people around you are great traders, they can really protect you and allow you to make money. But I think that for the average person, having little liquidity . . . I think it's very dangerous.

People are so into this buy and hold mentality, and it just doesn't work in this market right now. Last year I would say yes, start up with a small amount, but in this volatile market, I think the $25,000 you can easily kiss it good-bye in two or three trading days.

Q: How do you find most people usually get their start in direct access trading? I know it is different across the board. Just in general, what are the different types of people?

A: Most of the people I've met, it happens because they were disgruntled in their other jobs, or they weren't happy in their other jobs. Most of them came from trading something, perhaps. I used to be a currency trader for this Dutch bank in Chicago. The volatility in currency was just dying with the onset of the EMU, and it just wasn't really going anywhere, so I wanted to leave. My friends were in equities; they were saying that's where the volatility is. I'd just had enough of currency trading. I've met other people that came in after me, and they pretty much were sick and tired of their jobs as well.

Q: And not just traders?

A: Exactly. Bankers, lawyers, people in advertising. They come from all walks of life. And they come into day trading because they see it's good money, good hours, something a lot better than what they had at their previous jobs.

Q: Talking to a lot of the guys that talk about when you're starting off trading and what you should be doing, a lot of them talk about some kinds of simulators and trading programs. How effective are they, have you found? Is it worth it to go through them and to spend a week or 2 or 3 weeks or whatever it is, to the point where you're starting to interpret some of the moves and get a better understanding?

A: Definitely. I think it makes perfect sense to go into a training program. To start off, say, 1 week of just simulation. The name of the game is electronics. The fastest and first guy in is going to get the stock, so if you're not comfortable with the keys, or how different market makers control stocks, or how ECNs are going to control the price movement of stocks, you're going to get killed.

When I started, I spent a week just trying to learn the key strokes. I'm not a very good typist. I've seen people who are good typists and other people who aren't. Definitely the people who are good typists survive in this game. So you have to spend at least a week on simulations, and then when you do what they say, go live. Also, you need to be sitting with someone who's traded before.

I don't think I've ever met anyone who's just been thrown into the mix and has been very successful. Everyone who is successful will tell you he or she had a successful trainer who made a lot of money. So I think it's essential if you want to be a successful trader to get the training.

Q: There's obviously been so much attention in terms of just the Nasdaq stocks over the last couple of years with all that's happening. Just to make it clear, What are the advantages of trading stocks on the Nasdaq (besides the better technology available) over trading stocks on the NYSE?

A: Like you said, it's all electronic. It's a general, faceless product where whoever is the fastest is going to get the execution. There are some biases against day traders. You'll see that market makers will give preferences to other market makers, but that aside, the way the Nasdaq is set up, if I hit the SOES button, or if I preference the order first, I'm going to get it. I think that's essential.

The whole point of day trading is to be leveraged and to take advantage of momentum swings. So what you need is fast execution and reliable execution. If you do New York, your fills are dependent on the specialist. The specialist decides who buys and sells stock and at what price, so you really can't job the daily fluctuations. It's a lot tougher to do New York. But you'll never complain about Goldman Sachs and Yahoo! or Microsoft, or any of the big stocks. These market makers step up to the plate.

Q: What do you find are the main advantages you have over those who are sitting home on their Power E*TRADE or their Ameritrade or their online investing account?

A: A lot of things. One is being surrounded by other quality traders, which helps. I've tried to trade at home, remotes, in front of my TV, my computer. It's a lot more difficult in terms of getting a sense of the overall direction of the market or the stock.

When good traders surround you, it's a lot easier to see the overall picture. Unfortunately, there are also a lot of bad traders that shout things out at you, but you develop selective hearing. You tend to listen to what some of the traders say. I think that's one of the most important skills. That's why I make sure I get in to work every day instead of trading from home. I like being surrounded by intelligent people who trade.

Q: What about in terms of the execution?

A: The traders that I work with are all about speed rather than overall direction. Most of the guys in here, they're momentum traders. They hardly just sit down and say I'm going to buy because the thing's going up. They like to see strength and weakness. That's where execution is very important. If you buy and realize as soon as you buy you're wrong, you'll be the first guy to hit the bids and maybe even get short. Whereas if you're doing this online, yes, they offer level II, but you really can't feel the strength or the weakness or the momentum of the stocks. Most people who do it online are looking to buy, and then they go to work or they run out to the store 2 hours later, and if it's up, they sell it. That's nothing like what we do here. It's a very professional way of trading what these guys do.

Q: How does an individual without a lot of experience in the markets kind of catch up to the professionals who have the years of trading under their belts?

A: I don't think that's anything to worry too much about.

Q: Is it that the market's consistently changing, and it's who adapts to it best who succeeds?

A: I don't think you have to be intellectually smart to be a good trader. That's a misconception. I've been trading for a while, and I know other people who have been trading for a long time. It's about recognizing patterns. Markets are based on human behavior. It's actually humans buying and selling. It's being able to recognize that human behavior pattern.

You learn to see if there's a panic, if they're going to buy or sell it, and that basically only comes with experience. The more and more you're watching the stocks, the more you can recognize what's called price action. Does it go up $2 and come off a $1, or does it run up $5? Or does it go up a quarter, go down a half, then run up $5? Those patterns just become so recognizable over and over and over. Granted, yes, this market's been really crazy, and we haven't seen this for a while. Still, you can see the intraday moves, when a stock looks really weak, or if it looks really strong. That only comes with experience.

There are definitely some guys who just have the innate ability as great traders to recognize when it's going up or down. But you can take an average person off the street, if you just have the person watching the stock every single day for like a year, he or she is going to recognize that, for example, the bids aren't dropping, so maybe buy it because this thing's going up. That's how these guys are able to . . . like if a stock runs up $10, they're still willing to pay the offers because they know it's going to go up another $10.

You probably take a person who doesn't know, who will say, "It's already run up $10, I'm not going to buy it." But if people recognize these price patterns, they're not going to be afraid to buy it even though it's just run up. That comes with experience, not just guts.

Q: How did you first develop your trading strategy? And how does one go about defining one's own trading strategy?

A: Actually, I'd say about 80 percent of my style came from my boss at the Foreign Exchange. I basically spent 2 years as his assistant. He was the senior currency dealer at this bank that I was at. It was just 2 years of him riding me, telling me, "Why are you doing that, why are you buying, why . . . ?" It was just a beastly relationship, but he was a phenomenal trader, well known in the business, very profitable every year. So I was inspired to trade like him. He molded me to trade like him.

And I just trade what I learned in currency over at the Foreign Exchange. It's a different ballgame, but the disciplines are the same, the strategies are the same. I probably learned 80 percent from him.

Q: What was his strategy per se?

A: He's what's known as a fader. I don't know if you're familiar with that term. It's like when you fade moves. If it rallies up, you sell into it. It sells off, you're buying into it. You're basically hoping that it converges back to its average price.

So when I moved over to equities, it was tough because I moved over into one of the greatest bull runs where you literally, like I said, if it ran up 10 points, you still had to buy it. And it was difficult, because I was selling into those moves and I was losing a lot of money, while everyone else was just loading up; they didn't care. So I had a very hard time adjusting.

In currencies, if there was a 3 percent move, that was a huge, huge move. If you just faded that move, you would always make money. Whereas in equities, the stock can double in a day. It's really not a big move. So you think wow, the stock's just gone from $2 to $10! You're going to start shorting it. Well, what do you know, it's up at $20. Now you just lost everything. So I had to adjust to that.

That's where being around some other guys probably filled in a lot of blanks for me. Sitting next to smart traders expanded my trading disciplines to another level. But I'm basically trying to find a balance of both, of everyone's style. And I'm constantly redeveloping myself just to fit the market.

I think that's how most people end up. It's just through time that they develop their own style. I'm sure they get a lot of it from the people they sit around. You try to aspire to trade like the people who make a lot of money. If you see they're doing something right, you want to learn some of their techniques.

Q: What's a good way for somebody who's starting off to develop sort of a conservative trading strategy?

A: The easiest way is not to trade (*laughter*). I don't know. For a conservative style, you can stick to the stocks you know and not just jump into a stock that's flying around. Most of these guys around here, if it's running, they'll just get in and start pounding on it. I think that's a very dangerous way to get involved. If a stock is showing abnormal volume or price movement, these guys will just get in. I would suggest for a beginner not to get involved, especially if you don't know anything about the company.

A lot of these guys get in, and they don't know if it's, for example, an Internet, or a chip company, or whatever. I think that's sort of dangerous. You should know some of the basics and fundamentals behind each company before you just get in and start buying and selling.

I think if you play momentum, you're relatively safe. Momentum will always exist in markets. If you tend to buy in strength, you're all right, as long as you're taking quick profits. Quick profits, quick losses.

Risk/reward they're always talking about. Your reward should always be greater than your risk. It seems basic, but a lot of times you wind up finding that you're willing to risk 2 points just to make a half a point. That's very dangerous. A beginner who wants to make a point shouldn't be risking a point. That's just the basics of trading. Whatever you're trading, that's what they tell you—make sure the risk/reward is appropriate. That's what I would tell anyone who wants to stay conservative.

Q: With so much information out there, how do you go about filtering what's relevant for you in terms of what you should be trading or what you're interested in trading?

A: I have the benefits of having a Bloomberg and the Internet, so whenever I see a stock that seems to be trading heavily online, I always try to find out what the information is, and if there's any kind of fundamental changes behind the company.

The old adage: You buy the rumor, sell the fact. It still exists and probably will always exist. Sometimes you have to go against the stream. If everyone's buying this rumor and you know what the real event is, sometimes you might want to go against it. It's tough to say.

If I think it's just a fundamental change in the company, I tend to use that rather than just pure rumor momentum of the stock.

I don't tend to go by chat rooms. I mean I look at it because if 25 percent of the people out there are looking to chat rooms, I want to know why they're buying and selling, but I never, ever buy or sell on what someone says on a chat room. I think it's crap, and you can actually quote me on that. But a lot of people are very influential on those chat rooms, so people go on what they say.

If a stock is just moving out of whack, I'll check what the news is, Dow Jones, Reuters, Bloomberg. If I can't find anything there, I go to the chat rooms. Sometimes you get some good stuff, but I'll never buy into what someone says. I would suggest to anyone who wants to survive in this business not to go by what the chat rooms suggest.

Q: What about in terms of analysts' reports or the Fed? What are the other main things people should keep their eye on, so to speak?

A: I think the analysts are more for longer-term investors. It's good to know if you're playing a stock almost every day what the general sentiment of the analyst is. There used to be a point where analysts had a huge influence over a stock price, but I think we've realized not one person or institution is bigger than the market, so I don't think you can get too caught up in what an analyst says.

A perfect example was this QXLC. An analyst from I think it was Best mentioned Q, put a $1000 price tag on the stock. It was a $20 stock. It's basically an online auction site like E-Bay, but in Europe. The guy was calling it the E-Bay of Europe, with a $1000 price tag. It traded at $20. Before it opened up, it went from $20, literally in 5 minutes, right before they opened up, all the way up to $100. We were trying to find out exactly what his comments were, we couldn't find the news story, and David and I were thinking that this guy was full of it, so we got short up there. I mean, come on, $1000? I don't even know where the stock's trading now. Let's see, it's trading at $18, lower from where the analyst put that price tag.

We were showing at $100. You've got to take these analysts' opinions with a grain of salt.

There are some guys who are very influential. An obvious example would be the guy from Goldman Sachs for Microsoft. He basically controls the price of Microsoft. But by the time they say something, it's too late. You really can't trade off of it.

Q: Do you find that since you're at Tradescape or at an actual trading firm, you do have access to kind of better information, so to say, or more real-time information?

A: Yeah, but the real-time information is good for just pure momentum rather than long-term investing. It's all about timing for us, day traders. The people at home, if they're going to buy it and hold onto it for a week, I don't think they need the news in real time, but the real-time news I think is very important. A lot of times you see stocks spiking up or down and it's because of some news release. And because I'm sort of a contrarion, I like to buy into weakness or sell at the strength. If there's some kind of fundamental news, I want to know before I start loading up on it.

Q: You talked about chat rooms, and a lot of people talk about CNBC. But in terms of rumors and opinions you hear about, whether it's a TV show or whether it's other traders, how do you use that information?

A: It's like Joe Kernan. He has what I call the Joe Kernan factor. I'm sure you've noticed that. If he opens his mouth, or any of these analysts that come on open their mouths and talk up a stock, it's always good for some free money, as long as you're one of the first people in. If you're buying it at the top, you're going to get slaughtered. That's where if you're a quick typist, as soon as an analyst opens his or her mouth, you know the symbol, you type it up, and you just start playing the offers. That's honestly free money.

Some people at the firm, that's all they do. That's how they make their money. Fundamentally they're not changing anything about the stock, but if there are 10,000 other day traders out there who hit their buy buttons, it's going to send the stock up. So it's an easy way to make money, but in terms of a very short term play. Just because he says "We like the stock, we have it in our portfolio," you don't buy and hold it for the rest of the month. You just buy it, and as soon as you get it you sell it.

Honestly, in this market there is free money. You just have to know how to take it.

Q: Do you find yourself using more technical or fundamental analysis per se? Are you looking at charts? What are you using to determine which stocks you trade?

A: I think more in terms of momentum, but I also know the technicals. I look at charts. The charts are an easy way to get in and out of stock. They can help you realize that you have a good buy or a bad buy. Obviously I'm not going to know all the fundamentals of every single stock out there, but the 20 stocks that I look at every single day—I know the basic fundamentals.

I use the charts because half the traders out there in the world use charts. If they're all keying a certain level, I'm going to get in front of that level, I'm going to beat them to that punch. Even though in technical analysis it's not right, but if there's 50,000 people out there using charts, like I said, you have to adjust. You have to do what other people are doing as well. You have to be one step ahead of the market.

Q: How do you determine which are those stocks that you're trading? Are you looking for ones that are more active? Is it staying constant on a quarterly basis? How are you determining that?

A: I have two different ways to trade during the day. First, I'm more of a market player. Every day, every night I like to have a general direction of where the market's going, not only the following day, the entire day, the week, the month, the year. When I come into the office in the morning, the market may look like it's going to go up. I'll buy a handful of what are called market stocks—the Intels, the Ciscos, the Microsofts, the JDSUs. I'll buy maybe a little basket of stocks because I like the market. If I think it's going down, I'll short these stocks. I like doing that because it keeps me in the market. I can tell if it's strong or I can tell if it's weak. That's really the true way to gauge how strong a market is—if you've got some risk. Then there are stocks—maybe three or four—that just go crazy for one reason or another. Maybe there's some kind of news, or maybe just one big buy order or sell order. I'll get into that as well. Things that have unusual price movements or volume, I'll get into it.

Q: So you get in and try to find out what the news is?

A: Exactly. Before I start buying or selling anything, I'll jump into the market stocks because I'm just going off the market, but if it's some random stock that I've never traded, I pull up the charts, I try to pull up news, maybe some of the chat rooms and try to assess the situation like that.

Every single day, there are 5000 stocks in the Nasdaq. There's maybe three or four that just go out of whack. You basically want to jump into those.

Q: Is there ever a point when a stock is too volatile to trade? Is that ever a possibility?

A: Oh, yeah, definitely. There was a stock that was a perfect example. Literally in 2 days it went from like $100 up to like $600, which is crazy. The following day it was down 300 points. It's just an insane stock. There are stocks out there that I won't even look at.

When the Internets were really crazy, about a year and a half ago, I thought the same. I didn't want to play any of the Internets. I like to trade in size. I don't like playing a wide spread stock for like 100 or 200 shares, it's just not worth my time. And I don't want to play it for like 3000 shares. It's just not worth the risk/reward.

Q: Conversely, does it get to the point . . . when a stock is not moving enough for you to trade it?

A: If it's just . . . There's what's called noise, people buying and selling because of the natural orders that come in, or maybe someone trying to push it up. You can tell if it's just noise. I don't get involved. I look for trends, for example, if a stock's going up, or if it went up and then came back down. Those are the types of patterns I'm look-ing for—something that's trending or moving very sharply. Other-wise, if it's just going sideways, which I think the market probably does every few months, I try not to get involved.

Q: How much analysis do you do before you actually get in on a stock?

A: Actually, not that much.

Q: Take me through what you do per se or what happens in terms of you seeing a stock and pulling up the volume or whatever else you look at.

A: Right. If I see a stock that's in play, as I say, the first thing that I do is pull up the graph. I look at the news, and then maybe a little longer-term graph, going back 20 days, or back to a year, just depending on what the news is. That all involves. . . . If I don't see any news I'm very hesitant about, I mean I'll get in, but I'm hesitant about taking on size.

Since I'm a momentum player, that's what I'm basically going off of. If there's some news out there that I think is going to affect the price of a stock, that's when I'll start taking a position in it. Or if we see it break some huge technical levels, I'll start adding to the size.

But if I don't see anything to point me in one direction or the other, I'll just take my standard size and then try to play the momentum. If I buy and it only gives me half a point of profit, I'll take it. Whereas if I think the news is awesome and it stalls after a half point, I may not hit the bids. I'll think this can go up another two points. That's basically my whole thought process.

If I hit the bids and then the bids come right back, I might go and try to play the offers again. It's hard to say. It all comes down to mainly the momentum of the stock.

Q: Do you find you're biased in terms of the stocks you play, stocks you've heard of, or specific sectors that you like?

A: I'm not quite sure what. . . .

Q: For example, you mentioned a highly active stock or a stock you've heard of. Does it make it easier or harder to play per se, for example, stocks in the Internet or biotech sectors? Do you find that you're more drawn to those, or are you more drawn to the no-names that all of a sudden took a 200 percent pop?

A: I'm definitely more comfortable playing the stocks that I know. You're familiar with the price movement, the price action, you know who the big hitters are, who are the good market makers, what types of games they like to play.

If I just want to get in and buy Nasdaq, I'll buy the stocks that

I'm comfortable with. Today was a great day to just buy any strong Nasdaq stock. Intel was up $12. That's a great day for someone like myself. I play Intel almost on a regular basis. If it's up $12, that's like a gift for me. I play it every single day. I'm not going to try to buy a secondary stock, like a secondary chip stock, if I see Intel running up 12 points.

Q: Are you looking for specific things to happen in terms of a movement in Intel for when you get in, or is it more of a gut feeling on a chart, based on where it's going?

A: It's a combination of all of this. How strong the market is, that is, the overall market; how strong the chip sector is; and how strong Intel is. By gauging all three of those it determines what kind of size I'm putting on, what kind of risk I'm putting on, when I'm going to take profit. It's just sort of hard to say. There's no set formula on how I trade.

Q: Do you recommend for beginners to short stocks, and if so, in terms of how much money? That is, in comparison with what you do, versus what you would encourage beginners, people you train, to do.

A: I don't tell anyone to short stocks when they're starting out, except for the past 2 months; this has been the greatest bull market ever. It's just been a given in all the studies. The distribution of stock prices is skewed toward the upside.

In currencies, the price distribution was skewed toward the downside, like you'd always short the dollar because if you look back toward the eighties, the dollar was super strong against the yen. I don't know if you remember this, but it collapsed over the past 15 years. The yen used to be worth like 400 yen to a dollar; now it's worth 100. So that's why it was skewed to the downside, whereas equities, it's skewed toward the upside. Nasdaq and the Dow are going up 30 percent every single year. You can see it, especially in the way a lot of these guys trade. If a stock sells out, they're averaging all the way down. What do you know, 2 days later it comes all the way back and they make a killing.

Except for this past run here, some people have gotten beaten up, but one week, we hit a 500-point sell off. Well, we rallied back

500 points. That alone just shows you that it's sort of skewed to the upside. The way stocks move, as soon as someone goes high bid, everyone else joins the bid and then they start playing the offers. Or if someone low offers it, no one's hitting the bids. It's just so skewed to the upside. It actually makes me sick sometimes. But it's a lot easier to make money on the long side.

But I think playing on the short side is an essential strategy that you're going to have to learn how to do. Once a year we always go into a bear turn of the market. Last year it was around August and October. The year before it happened at the same time. This year it's right now.

There are times when you want to beat up the short stocks. It just goes on these ridiculous runs. But other times, those are the times when you're going to lose your shirt.

Q: Do you use any sort of mental rules for discipline in terms of where you'll get out on a position if it's not going your way?

A: That's all in terms of how much pain I want to sit through. It varies. If it goes down half a point, I'm smacking the bids. Sometimes I let it go 10 points against me. You always try to tell yourself to be disciplined. The great traders are disciplined. Sometimes you just let yourself go because you're in a bad mood or you just become so stubborn. I always try to tell myself I have certain risk levels that I'm willing to deal with. I'd say the majority of the time I stick to them.

It's not only a monetary amount but also a price movement amount that I try to key. Basically I look at my trade; I say, What am I hoping to make, and what am I willing to lose? Does it make sense, that risk/reward tradeoff? If I'm holding it down 2 points against me, it's because I figure I can make at least 2 points on the upside. But if I'm holding it 2 points against myself and I only wanted to make a half point, then I feel really bad. I'm totally un-disciplined, and I get mad.

Q: When you enter a trade, what are you looking to see based on when you're ready to enter or exit the trade? In terms of whether it's been a good trade, you made the money you wanted to make, it's time to get out?

A: It's just the price action of the stock, the strengths of the bids versus the strengths of the offers. Recognizing what the market makers are doing is also really important.

Usually, in every stock there're always one or two guys who can control the price. So you want to pick that out about the stock, who that market maker is. You tend to sort of make sure, keep an eye on it. If the guy's on the offer, I'm going to be looking to sell it too. I mean, he or she may be playing games, obviously. The market maker may be like a bid, some other ECN bid, but I'm not going to try to read into it. Or if the guy's on the bid and it looks good, I'm not going to be quick to hit the bids.

But now it seems to be getting away from the market makers. It seems to be more the ECNs. The Island and Instinet are getting more involved about pushing on stocks. I'm always trying to keep an eye out on that. The problem is it creates so much noise, especially through Island. People playing games, or flash a large bid or a large offer just to play games with it. You just sort of have to sift through all that information.

I put more weight on the market makers than like Island itself. But you also have to be aware of the ECNs.

Q: Take me through the opening and closing of markets, often the hottest times. How do you go into that in terms of your strategy?

A: For the open, a lot of it was yesterday's closing, or how the market finished, or if there was any overnight news. What you tend to see a lot is that all the morning orders come in, so you want to take advantage of that. All the retail orders come in, or the funds are buying and so on, so you want to be quick to notice where the strength is, who's buying it, who's selling it.

If I realize Goldman Sachs is on the bid, I'm going to take the chance and get long with it, just for the opening orders. I think it's a great way to make money, just because there tends to be that overexaggeration. A fund's coming in buying, well all the day traders are going to push it up against him and keep pushing it up.

Then you see that toward the close. All the retail orders come in for the close, or the market makers are finishing up their day orders. So you would like to try to make sort of an educated guess in terms of if it's going to finish strong or weak.

Also, a lot of it, I think, for the end of the day is a little more dependent on what happens during the day. Usually you can tell if it's strong that it's going to usually stay strong. If it's weak, it's going to stay weak. That works the majority of the time. Not all, but you always like to keep that in the back of your mind.

Q: How do you update your strategy over time as the markets are changing month to month, year to year? How do you kind of stay on top of your game?

A: You find yourself trying to do other stuff like you get into the same routine every day. You play the same stocks; you trade the same way. Once you realize you're not making the money you should be making, you start doing other things.

It's almost like a day-to-day reevaluation. I like to go home every day and think about what I did well and what I did wrong, what I'm going to do next time if I see the exact same thing. That way it's always a dynamic strategy. You're always changing it. Your disciplines are going to stay the same, but you recognize that pattern—like I said, we are recognizing patterns. Today was such a great bull run, there were so many times when I should have just been buying, but I was just a little more hesitant. I felt maybe we might have a last minute sell-off, but we didn't. When I recognize that again, I'm just going to buy into the close. It's like that.

Q: Any last words of advice for someone getting into it?

A: I actually think it's going to get tougher. Nasdaq is imposing all these changes. It is supposed to reduce the volatility. Nasdaq is not supportive of the day trader. It's trying to protect market makers and the retail people, not traders like us. So I think it's a tough racket, and it's just going to get tougher. As more and more people get into it, it's going to be harder to make money.

Q: What about the technology behind it in terms of the direct access? How do you see people generally, even online investors, starting to use that?

A: I think that's probably going to be the wave of the future. Cutting out the middleman has always been the American way. As we see that people more educated about the markets and about how Nasdaq and New York and how the exchanges work, I think they're going to want more control. Americans have always wanted more control, more power, more space, more bang for the buck. That's why we're always getting faster and bigger cars. People want bigger apartments. They're going to want more control over their fills. They're going to be able to think they can outsmart the brokers. I don't know if that's necessarily good or bad, but I definitely think you're going to see a lot more people using direct access.

Unfortunately, they may get hooked on it, which could be bad. But I think it's a whole positive thing like what Tradescape's doing with its online brokerage. I think that's going to attract a lot of people who use E*TRADE. I don't use any of the online brokers, but I've heard people complain about their execution. Everyone's complaining about everything.

I think the best way to shut people up is to let them control their own execution.

INTERVIEW TWO

Q: Is it even realistic to expect to make money in the markets, where there are so many sophisticated traders and institutions trading day in and day out?

A: Well, I think that one can expect to make a reasonable rate of return on almost any well-diversified portfolio, in terms of general investing. Sophisticated people are not usually looking to make a normal rate of return, because they can't support their level of sophistication on that. That is, if you're some big bank, you handle large accounts, you need a lot of talent to run these accounts, and to pay them, you had better be making some money from your portfolios. The problem is when you see the average Joe trying to pull down eight figures from something he read in a chat room. That's unfortunate; things don't work that way. Even big institutions don't try that stuff; they aren't gambling, why should the small guy?

Initially, I think there were some people making extraordinary returns from online investing, but that free lunch didn't last. If an investor jumps in with both feet and tries to work hard, sure, there is money to be made, but by then the investor has earned it through hard work, not through some magical tree that money grows on.

Q: With a small amount of investment capital, how much of a return can a beginner expect, or should anyone even expect to make money in the beginning?

A: At the beginning the investor should try to not lose money. And at the beginning I would hope that the investor had a small amount of investment capital. Giving someone a lot of money to invest with at the beginning is like giving a child a loaded gun. You're just making the losses bigger. It is better to start out slow and not make the mistakes more expensive than they have to be. I think that if someone can pull off a couple or three quarters without a loss, and employing a well-thought-out strategy, then they are learning, forget about making money. It's losing money that should worry the beginner.

Q: Is it safer for an individual to turn to a stock market professional rather than go it alone in the markets?

A: I don't think that the stock market professionals that an individual can realistically turn to really have that much more to offer. I think a lot of the reasons were outlined in this book. It's just too hard to find the kind of investment advice that one is looking for, given the fees that some of these places charge. This is, of course, a generality, and like all generalities, it should be taken with a grain of salt. I know many talented individuals working in the field with creative and great investment ideas. Unfortunately, I don't know many willing to dole this advice out to the average Joe. If that's the case, it may be time to think about going it alone and educating yourself a little; it can save a ton.

I remember a good old friend of mine I hadn't seen in years came up to me and told me a story about his recent investment experience. It turns out the guy had some money in a couple of funds, and they were just dogs. He tells me that some guy was going to represent him, from one of the big firms, I forget which. The point is, his new broker was going to visit him at his home that night. Luckily, I caught him before he went ahead with the sales pitch. I asked him one question: What are the credentials of the individual to whom you would hand over your nest egg for investing? He laughed and said that the man had owned some sort of resort before doing this and then had taken a course somewhere, and

God knows what else. I couldn't believe it! I explained to him that there was no need to get hosed on $50+ commissions and heaven knows what else comes down his way.

Q: How much money does a small investor realistically need to bring to the table to participate in direct access trading?

A: I don't know the answer to that, because the systems are so new. If I had to set a minimum, it would have to be based on the minimum commission, and so on, and the cost of information from these systems. There is definitely a fixed cost to being involved in direct access trading. The more trades you make, I think, the more economical it becomes per trade. It's the same deal as an all-you-can-eat buffet; the more you can pack in, the more of a deal it is to go to one. That doesn't mean that it doesn't make sense to not go to a buffet if you aren't ready to stuff your face, though. You don't have to be an eating machine, and going to one can still be worth your while.

There is also a more important issue to keep in mind. This stuff looks like it's here to stay. Twenty years ago if you asked the same question about "computers," maybe the answer would have been that for it to make sense that someone go out and buy a computer, they should be some sort of a businessperson, or who knows what. But as computers have become cheaper and more commonplace, now we have them in little boxes on the palms of our hands. So the same can be said for direct access trading. Setting a figure as to how much one needs to invest using this technology is irrelevant, because I think that sooner or later everyone will invest using this technology. It is superior, and the costs of using it will fall, as has the cost of all superior technology. It's just a question of getting the critical mass of users for this to spread.

Q: What are the realistic gains that the direct access investor can hope to take away from the stock markets if they are not going to be a full-fledged day trader?

A: Perhaps the gains of a direct access investor can't be expressed directly, like, say, 10 percent a year, or something, but rather in the benefit of direct access per trade. That is, given that the investor uses direct access, he or she can buy at a low point and get out at a high point in the movement of the stock price, and these small gains may represent an extra percentage point or two per stock. This could add up significantly, depending on the size of the portfolio. Also, the management of the portfolio is much more precise with direct access trading. These are the types of gains that someone who is not day trading can still benefit from; it's like online investing, but with more accuracy and precision.

Q: How do people usually get their start in direct access trading?

A: I think some people have a natural tendency to get into this type of thing, and sometimes it works out, and sometimes it doesn't. There are all kinds of technology buffs and former Wall Street employees involved in this, because they see the profits being reaped by Wall Street first hand and want their slice of the pie. Traders from other markets sometimes come over as well. There are also people who try their hand at one thing or another until they can find their niche. I'll tell you, though, they all have one thing in common, which is the entrepreneurial spirit of sorts that some individuals carry and drives them. There is no easy living to be made here, but it is certainly interesting. If you want something else, try being a librarian.

Q: How realistic and effective are simulators and other training programs for traders and small investors? Are they worth the effort, or are the true learning experiences where one gets one's hands dirty in the markets?

A: I think the simulators are invaluable. There used to be a trend in this business to trade on paper or to practice trading by watching the screen and writing down what you would have done, and so on. What a mess! You don't know how disappointing and inaccurate it can be to try to do things the old-fashioned way and not see them work out. I'll tell you, trying to follow the markets on paper is a chore, and doing your own charts, forget about it.

A simulator solves all these problems. It gives the individual something to practice on so they don't go in the first day and think, hey what's this button for? Oops! There goes $10,000! Just for that, the simulators are worth their weight in gold. But beyond that, they give the investor familiarity with the product they are going to use throughout their investing process. I think it's a win-win situation for the maker's of the product as well. Who wants to see a customer give up using your product because they are unfamiliar with it? And what's more, the better the trader, the more they will trade, so why not let them learn on the simulator? Trying to learn on paper is insane; it's like trying to copy the bible over by hand, without even a word processor. There's no gain.

Practicing on a simulator helps the individual learn how a stock moves and to test out their initial strategy. Of course, one really always has the safety net there because it's not real money that is on the line. That's part of the process too; the idea of the simulator is that the times when you really lose money, which will be the times when you really learn, will be less costly because maybe you won't make dumb mistakes that you made on the simulator. When the individual uses real cash instead of the simulator and trades, then they will have to know the limitations of their strategy and so on. Breaking the rules and picking the wrong stocks on the simulator are cost-free, but at least you can see what the consequences are, and then maybe you won't do it with real money.

Q: What advantages are there in trading Nasdaq stocks, say, over stocks listed on the NYSE?

A: Listed stocks are just tough; specialists are killers. And the volatility is zero, the limit order book takes precedence, the specialist has a clear picture of the market, it's no place for trading in and out of stocks. Leave that to someone else. The long-term potential of listed stocks is of interest to many investors, however. The blue chips are there, and many good companies are on the NYSE, so if the idea is to invest for the long haul, that may be the place to turn to. There is certainly a perception of less risk among some of the financial news people about listed stocks. I don't buy it, though; I think one should look at them on a case-by-case basis, because there are plenty of Nasdaq stocks that are as stable as some listed stocks.

Q: What kinds of information should the small investor or an individual with some capital sitting in a bank account or money market account take into consideration when looking at whether to enter the markets? What are the advantages of direct access trading, brokered trading, or mutual funds?

A: The average Joe with four paychecks in the bank should consider what the uses of this money are. If he is going on vacation in 3 months, then he should not tie his money up in the markets. This is just common sense. Some people talk about investing $1000 and turning it into $100,000 like the famous example we all know, but I probably shouldn't mention by name to keep the book politics-free. But that's just unrealistic; I mean, the general public should not expect to pull that off. So the first pieces of information that the small investor would need would come from himself or herself. What are the goals for the money? It's not the same to invest for retirement than for a car 2 years from now. It's not even the same to invest for retirement when you're 25 than when you're 55.

Money market accounts are great. The Internet has opened up a bunch of new opportunities for people who are interested in money market mutual funds, and so on; they are just all over the place, and you can scoop them up like they were ice cream cones. These are pretty short-term and risk-free, and what more could you ask for? But if you want to make some serious money, like for a college education, a money market account is not the best way. You can just outperform that with a couple of mutual funds. And so why not? Brokered trading is tough to argue for, because of the inexpensive alternatives that exist. If it were 10 years ago, I might have told a different story, but today there is just too much out there to go to a broker and give away $50. Just send the money you would have given to the broker to charity if your need to give money away that bad.

Q: How does an individual without a lot of experience in the markets catch up to professionals who have years of trading under their belt?

A: Well, the individual has to deal with the fact that there are going to be people out there who are better than him or her always and everywhere. Even people who began later than him or her and have less experience may turn out to be better traders. The goal is not to beat the Jones's but rather to be something you can live with. Who enters this game thinking that they are going to outperform Warren Buffet? Just work on outperforming your own expectations, and maybe you'll get somewhere.

Q: What is a trading strategy, and how does a small investor devise one?

A: A trading strategy is kind of a set of rules by which one guides one's decision process when trading. In the heat of the moment, one doesn't want to face a difficult decision without some guidance, just like one wouldn't coach a football game without a game plan. It's the same exact idea. Trading strategy, investment strategy, trading plan, people all call it different things. It just means thinking about what one wants to accomplish in the markets. Without this, even spectacular results can seem small, because there is no benchmark, no reference point. There is a need for a sense of accomplishment. I imagine one can get along without it, if it were necessary, but I don't know if it's possible to be a good investor without a sense of losses. That is the other side of the coin. A trading strategy includes rules to cut losses, to unwind positions, and to get out of dog stocks and worthless investments. Also, with a realistic plan, there is a realistic goal. And if one has a realistic goal, and it is not met, then it's time to reevaluate investments and think about what is going wrong. Even if you aren't taking in losses, if you aren't meeting the goals of your trading strategy, and the goals are not way out there in terms of ambition, then maybe there are some opportunities going unnoticed or there are some stocks that need to be dumped. A stock doesn't always need to lose money for an investor to dump it.

Q: When considering a trading strategy, how conservative should a small investor be in the beginning?

A: That really depends on the person. There are some people who are very risk averse and just don't like to worry about what is happening to their money. There is a huge tendency these days to watch the market and the swings in the Dow, and the S&P500, or some other index. If you are not the money manager for some mutual fund, who cares? Some people ask me if they should be worried that the market fell some odd amount of points today or rose some odd amount of points another day. Unless they are selling the next morning, one-day swings don't really affect everyday people who are in the markets for 10- or 20-year horizons. Unfortunately, however, many people don't realize this and worry about their money at all times. At 30 years from retirement they're worried about their savings. Obviously, these people need not be conservative because they may lose all their money; they need to be conservative so that they can get some sleep at night. It's a quality-of-life issue for them, not an investment issue. The personal costs of bearing the risk is just too much, not because the stock is too risky, but because they perceive the risk to be greater than it actually is. And all the financial news programs that they listen to just make it worse in some cases.

In general, I have seen younger people get aggressive with their stocks and do well. That makes a lot of sense, and when I say young, I mean 15 or 20 years from retirement. In a way, some people are not taking advantage of some great investment opportunities because of apathy. But, perhaps they are some of the ones that have the quality-of-life issues, and they are better off not getting involved if they are going to fret too much over the markets. Others, however, just don't know about what's available and are often not trading at all. They need to get aggressive, but not about any one particular investment, just about investing in general.

Q: With the glut of market information available to the small investor, where and how does one go about filtering what is relevant? How much of it is included in the trading strategy?

A: Well, I think there are a couple of easy rules for filtering information and incorporating it into an investment plan. The main rule is that if something sounds great, it probably is wrong. That's just common sense, especially when it comes to hot tips about stocks and whatnot. There is no reason to think that any of what one hears is true. If something was free and readily available to everyone, like a stock tip given on a TV show, then maybe it's not such a good idea to use it. Good information isn't free because if it were, it would cease to be good information. If finding something out takes a lot of work and thinking, then it may have potential, since that will usually be the road less taken by investors. Mainly, I would include this type of information into the trading strategy. This doesn't mean take the hard route for everything; it means learn everything that is free and easy, since everyone will already know that stuff, and then if you manage to get some edge through hard work, that may be the edge that pays off. The free stuff everyone knows, so working hard to learn that doesn't make a lot of sense.

Q: How does the small investor incorporate wide information and statistics on the economy as a whole, where this information is not generally aimed at one stock or another (e.g., consumer price index figures or Fed interest rate hikes)?

A: These baseline statistics are very useful, especially for the small investor who is not actively involved in the markets on a day-to-day basis. The movements in the CPI or the Fed's interest rate policy tend to be big movers in the economy, and this can affect everyone, whether you are involved in the markets or not. If the Fed starts tightening interest rates to slow the economy down, people may lose jobs. These individuals may not be investors looking to beat the S&P500; they may be just average people working somewhere. As the economy slips into a recession, it is important to know what is going on. Suppose one was looking to buy a home or something, it may not be the best time if you're unemployed in something very procyclical like home construction, when the economy is going into a recession. New car purchases and this type of thing, people need to be aware of what is going on; they can't just be oblivious to the general economic activity of the country until it's too late and then start asking questions about what happened to all their economic well-being. These general figures are the ones that will indicate the situation of the economy as a whole.

There are some basic economic relationships that are reflected in these numbers; they are the kinds of guidelines that investors use to see what's going on, the big picture so to speak. When these numbers come out, everyone readjusts how the big picture is looking in their minds, and the markets react. Sometimes the market can anticipate what the numbers will say, in which case the adjustment is not so great. For the average investor, these numbers can signal when to get into or out of the stocks that they are in. It's all a question of how long you want to wait and when is the right time to get out. If you're going to need money within a matter of months or a year, these numbers can get to be very important, because they can signal where the economy is headed in that time. Recently, the interest rates have become a favorite of Wall Street investors. They look to Alan Greenspan to see where he's pushing the economy toward and keep an eye on his comments to Congress, the minutes to his meetings, and so on. Some people even try to guess which way he'll push rates by how thick his briefcase is or the color of his tie. Investors can get very creative when they have money on the line; it can get pretty amusing sometimes. In the end, everyone wants to know what these big statistics are saying because they are the bird's-eye view of the economic activity of the country, which is where we are putting our dollars.

Q: What are some sources of information that are useful for small investors who may not be full-time day traders but who still want to use direct access trading?

A: There are many sources. I think that the financial newspapers are OK, and financial magazines as well. Many people read *Investor's Business Daily* or the *Wall Street Journal.* These are very thorough sources for investment news. They cover the basics every day. I have my favorite sources, but I don't want to play favorites and advertise them, because what one reads is more a question of personality than the source itself. Some people find *Investor's Business Daily* and the *Wall Street Journal* unbearable; others can read the newspapers even though they don't have a dime in the markets. Using direct access trading, it helps to have a source that can give one conditions for the market and some fairly recent updates. For that reason, newspapers and magazines are mainly for background. If one wants to know what is going on, there are sources online, and television programs going 24 hours a day, that are constantly spewing the very latest that they can find out about news and so on. These types of sources are very useful for small investors who need to keep up and get a quick look at what is going on for some stocks or some segment of the market. There are plenty of useful Web sites around with news on them, and of course, there are premium news subscription services for the hard-core investors who don't want to find out that they were the last ones to hear about something.

People using direct access trading can really decide up to what point they wish to keep up on the markets, because they have the alternatives of trading efficiently at high frequencies, which are not available to other investors. If they are not full-time day traders, what they can do is really focus on the stock that they trade, whether it be for the medium term or for the longer term, and watch closely for any warning signs. A difference of a few days can cost an investor if they aren't paying attention to the markets when big changes come. For these individuals, the financial press and television programs, and the Web sites are useful for complementing the technical information from their direct access brokers.

Q: What should a small investor be looking for in the markets when looking for a promising stock for the medium to long run?

A: I think in the medium to long run one should be looking for growth opportunities in stocks. There are the usual set of indicators for value stocks and so on which many investors swear by, but really these should complement common-sense intuition about the stock that one is investing in. People forget that in the long run what one is really investing in is the economic growth of the company and the sector that one buys stock in. It's difficult to argue that a company can be overvalued for 10 or 15 years; if that is the case, then it's time to reconsider the technique used for valuing stocks. It's just not rational that something be overvalued and yet able to sustain it's value for a decade in a market like the ones we trade in. For that reason, the value in companies has to come in the form of true growth in the company and the profits. It's also important to keep in mind that in the long run economic conditions can influence a company strongly, much more so than in the short run. For example, a company can be turning a profit now and may do so for a few years, but if what the company produces is worth less every day, then that company needs to either adapt to different markets or it will go out of business. This occurs sometimes with companies that specialize in products that become obsolete in a few years' time. A lot of people say that this is what drives the growth in Internet companies. No one is really sure of what the next generation of companies and industries will look like, because we are introducing a new medium for connecting and communicating and for reaching businesses, households, everything. This can change a lot of the landscape for how business is done, and it's already happening. Online investing is a perfect example of this. Anytime you introduce some new technology, the invention represented by this technology is useful for alleviating some problem, and this will most likely make the old way of alleviating the problem obsolete. In the past people turned to other more expensive ways of investing, and now they have this superefficient medium of investment for small amounts, especially compared with what some people out there were charging in the eighties. Now a lot of those high-priced investment places are learning to adapt or looking for work. This type of destruction and creation of jobs and industries occurs all the time in the economy. When looking for long-term investments, it is imperative to not sink money into a technology or business that is on the way out. That's when you get into trouble.

Q: What purpose do the rumors and opinions generated by financial television shows serve for the direct access trader? What use are they for the direct access trader?

A: Well, I sometimes listen to these programs, but not religiously. It depends, and it really is difficult to generalize, because there are some good analysts, and there are lots of people who are getting lucky or shooting darts and appearing on TV as well. As far as rumors, probably the small investor couldn't care less, unless they are day trading. One should be careful of rumors if they are day trading because the movement of the stocks need not be in the expected direction. It depends on if enough people bought into the idea that people believe the rumor, and how many people know by the time you hear about it, who is looking to benefit from spreading it—it's really a big mess. Serious day traders are weary of these things and try to use them as opportunities with a careful retreat always waiting. The others, who are not too short-term-minded, probably don't care about the rumors unless they are very serious ones, like the CEO has been pumping the stock and cooking the books or something really strange like that. If that's the case, the rumor will become news and spread like wildfire, and besides, these types of events don't happen everyday for most companies out there. Sometimes, for beginners, financial television shows really bring out some good topics, and people discuss interesting side topics such as retirement options and strategies for lowering taxes, sheltering money from estate or inheritance taxes, college savings, all sorts of things. The litigation of investments can get complicated. I don't think that too many of these programs will solve people's tax problems, but on more than one occasion I've seen important issues raised that perhaps would not occur in the minds of the typical investor out there. There are many instruments and options that people may not know even exist, and these programs can inadvertently open up people's horizons in that way.

Q: How does one approach the issue of forecasting stocks and estimating future stock prices? Is this realistic and appropriate for direct access traders?

A: Everyone is different on that issue because the answer is that no one is really cleaning up out there with perfect forecasts. At least, we would like to think this; perhaps someone is, and they are keeping their mouth shut and going unnoticed while they mint their own money with their forecasts of markets. I remember a friend of mine in the business was asked by a client what percentage of their savings should be in the markets. This client of his was very young, and my friend suggested that he get aggressive and invest in some growth stocks and take some well-thought-out risks to try and gain a higher return over the long term. The client curiously asked how much the stock portfolio would be worth in 10 years and how much the Dow would be in 10 years. Common! The investment strategy will hopefully get you someplace better, but the probability of hitting numbers in a 10-year horizon is nil. That's worse than asking what the winning lottery number will be; at least with lotto people have a chance of getting it right.

It's certainly good to have a short-run forecast of where stocks are moving; having one is equivalent to making an investment decision. In the long run, however, the idea is to look at the strength and health of the company and let the stock forecasts come in where they may; none will be correct anyway.

Q: What are some useful leading indicators for stock performance; i.e., what should one look at for selection of a stock to invest in or trade?

A: One of the most immediately useful indicators of stock performance is changes in volume, because you are talking about how much interest is in the stock. This can be crucial for the direct access trader trying to stay on top of a company. They will be the first to know when volume is increasing and the stock is starting to move. I've seen people do well with a strategy where they stay on a stock and watch for volume volatility. Other indicators can be the typical ones that investors use, P/E ratios and things like that. You know one time I saw something so incredible, it was a report on what people use as indicators of stock performance, and there are some people out there who use some scary stuff. The Internet craze for investment has brought some real eclectic people to the table. I say good for them if they are doing well, but I just hope they aren't showing up with their grandmother's retirement and blowing it on their feelings, or reading tea leaves or something. The most striking part of the report was that they showed evidence of people just jumping randomly on bandwagons for one stock or another. It turns out that, for example, on days when a stock was hot or there was some IPO or something that really stirred interest in the stock, other companies with similar ticker symbols would have intense volatility as well. For example, if some company named DOE on the market was trading like crazy because it was some JohnDoe.com or some new Internet craze, then similarly named companies would be trading as well. Suppose there was some company with a ticker symbol DEO or something; they would trade heavily on those days as well, and their price would move tremendously. It's this type of thing that is disturbing. I suppose that one could argue that it is wise to trade those stocks because there are people out there buying or selling them by mistake and one can make a profit off them. I don't know about that, however. It's too much like mindless gambling; betting on other people's mistakes has never been something that I would advise. What's worse are the people who are buying these stocks by mistake. Where would they get this sort of information that they can't even get the ticker symbol correct of the company that they would pour their savings in? What if these geniuses are trading on margin? I can't imagine how one could trade stocks in such a fashion. Perhaps they get their information from some Internet chat room or someplace. Imagine explaining to someone that you not only lost all of your savings, but also that you owe $10,000, just to close your account with the broker because you were trading on margin. And the reason you lost? You got the ticker symbol wrong on the stock that you wanted to buy!

Q: At what point is a stock too volatile to trade, or does a point such as this even exist?

A: I would have to say that that point doesn't really exist, except in the mind of the investor. There literally is no point at which a stock is too volatile to trade, as long as there are buyers and sellers. In some markets, big swings will cause the trading on the stock to halt; I don't know that too many people want to see that kind of volatility in the markets, because of the uncertainty it introduces. I'm sure day traders benefit from the volatility, and long-term investors are probably not concerned about local volatility when their money is in a stock for another few years. The main concern is for anyone looking to get their money out of the market during the period of high variation in the price of the stock. In this sense, direct access can help tremendously to manage the potential losses or gains from the volatile market. Some people day trading keep a window in their trading screen of active movers so that they can hunt these stocks out and trade them. The speed of execution allows them to maintain a safety zone where if in the midst of the volatility the stock price moves too far against them, they have a quick exit. It is for this reason that short-term investors using direct access can worry less about the volatility in some stocks.

It is well known that once a stock becomes volatile, it will stay volatile for a while, and once it becomes tranquil, it will stay tranquil for a while. This helps many people decide what they should be doing and what they should be looking for in terms of trading a volatile stock or not. If the stock has been trending for a while and something triggers a movement, the stock may begin to bounce around for a while. Stock prices do this all they time; they fluctuate for periods of time, and then they trend quietly for a period without much volatility at all. People have different ideas about why this happens; some say it's pent up pressure from the trending that brings the large fluctuations, but there are many plausible reasons. When investors see this beginning, they know to expect this cyclic pattern. That is, they know that there are periods of high and low volatility; whether the periods are longer or shorter is another question. However, the fact remains. Looking at this, investors are able to back out when they don't want to face volatility or, conversely, when they don't want to sit on a low-volatility stock, whether it be trending or moving in some general direction.

Q: When facing the thousands of stocks available for trading, is it even realistic to expect analysis to play a role in selection? Is one biased toward companies one has heard of or heard about? Is one biased toward one sector or another because of the herd mentality that draws so many investors to the same place? Are these biases bad for small investors, and if so, how do they guard against them affecting their trading decisions?

A: The thousands of stocks that are available are a kind of lottery of investment. Add to that the bulletin board stocks that people also buy, penny stocks, and others. It's a mine field out there. I think it's crucial to try to analyze every stock that one buys, because there is just too much at stake to be picking a random stock. There are some alternatives that have a pleasant outcome for those who wish to avoid learning about companies, profits, and so on. One is a mutual fund, where the investor can leave the learning to someone who works in the area all the time. These are interesting; they have some interesting strategies, and sometimes they actually work. A mutual fund is not a panacea of investment uncertainty, however. These guys put their pants on one leg at a time, just like the rest of us. By going to a mutual fund the investor is not avoiding or beating the problem, but just hoping that in the mine field of thousands of investment opportunities out there, the mutual fund does a better job at investing. The problem is that while it makes sense that the mutual fund will do better because it has better information, and so on, it also have many constraints that investors don't have and has to deal with problems that a small investor can avoid. Some of these problems are simply related to the size, and the issues that having billions of investment dollars can bring up, that a small investor (unfortunately) never has to worry about. It is in this vein that people simply turn to index funds. The idea is that while person A may know about some company and person B knows about some other company, it is difficult to argue that there are lots of people out there who know about every company. What an index fund does is exploit this fact, i.e., exploit the fact that there is no possible way that people can have an informational advantage on thousands of different companies involved in different sectors. An index fund comes in and buys a little bit of each stock and simply forms a market portfolio. By placing a little bit of their bet on every stock, or a large number of stocks, I should say, they are neutralizing the informational disadvantages that they may face relative to one investor or another. This way, index funds let people battle among themselves, and the index takes the average. The advantage is that they are never below average, but they are also never above average. They position themselves so that they are average by definition. In this way, they don't worry about informational advantages or having to research any companies from among the thousands available.

Q: Where is the line between selecting a stock on a gut feeling and making an impulsive trade? How does the small investor decide that his or her instinct is guiding him or her toward a successful trade?

A: The rules are very important for this type of decision. I don't know of too many people who would take time out of their day to tell someone they know that the investment they are doing is unwise, because there is just too much at stake. There are some things that I've noticed people don't criticize each other about too much, and investment strategies are definitely one. There was a guy I knew that was buying some real dogs, and he had some sort of system in mind where they would bounce back according to some seasonal mark or some month. It wasn't necessarily outrageous; I don't know if it could have worked under different circumstances, but he was overexposed, in my opinion. The problem is just that, however. What could my opinion possibly have to do with another individual's trading strategy? We're all big kids now, and no one needs the guy next to them telling them what to do. This person started in on these dog stocks and wouldn't let up, and finally, by the time he had unwound his position, he was down $300,000. That's tough. Again, I'm speaking in retrospect, and I respect this individual; he's no dummy. The reason someone can lose that kind of money is because he has it to lose from other successful trades. Things didn't go his way this time, and that's unfortunate. However, they have gone his way in the past, and there is no way anyone is going to tell him anything. It just doesn't happen; it's unprofessional. For this reason, rules are the saviors of the trader and investor. What you have to invest is what you have to protect. Investment is part making money grow and part hoping that money doesn't shrink. But one has to sit and write down a plan that includes lowering the probability of losing money to a tolerable size. With this, you have a rule of thumb for guarding against losses. You can't sit in the middle of a trade and reevaluate your entire portfolio for the next 10 years. So you make a rule of thumb and live with it. This will always help control losses; it's essential because there aren't many other signals that losses are mounting or that risks are too high. And then, of course, the rule should be followed. When the gut feeling is driving the investment, you may find yourself wandering away from the guidelines that you set out. These gut feelings are no good for beginners who are looking to preserve their money and watch it grow. After a trader is experienced, then he knows whether he wants to deviate from some rule or not, but more importantly, an experienced trader knows and is ready to face the possible consequences from doing so.

Q: What is a margin account, and should a small investor consider trading on margin?

A: A margin account (in case I've mentioned it already, it's good that we make clear what we mean) is when we trade using borrowed money. It's similar to taking out a loan and then buying stocks with the money. Anyway, these accounts are useful for individuals who wish to watch their initial investment grow by a very large rate very quickly. That is, they want to make a lot of money fast. Of course, this comes at the expense of the higher risk faced by the investor because of the possibility of losing money very fast. How this works is that an investor may invest, say, $100, and just put it into a stock. If the stock pays off a return of 7 percent, the investor made $7. Now, suppose the investor opened a margin account, with a 10 percent margin. Then, his or her $100 can now be up to 10 percent of the actual amount invested. As a result, the person can invest the same $100, but in reality, he or she can buy $1000 worth of stock, because 100 is 10 percent of 1000. Now the individual has a highly leveraged position. If the stock makes the same 7 percent, the individual gets $70 instead of $7. As a result, he or she gets a 70 percent return on his or her initial $100 investment. That is how a margin account works. Notice, however, that there are many complicated issues when dealing with a margin account. People should really find out what they are getting into when trading on margin. If, for example, one buys a stock on margin and the value falls, then the total investment value fell, and the company that loaned the money will demand more cash up front. That is called a *margin call,* and margin calls are notorious for devastating traders. I think small investors are wise to stay away from margin accounts at the beginning, when they are not too familiar with how things work in the stock market. Afterwards, if they choose to tolerate that level of risk, then they can certainly benefit from margin trading like any other investor. So long as they understand the risks.

Q: The openings of the market can be chaotic. What are some strategies for small investors in the market openings?

A: Yes, the openings are pretty bad. They can be chaotic and uncertain for everyone, not just small investors. I would recommend that people stay away from there in general. If you are a long-term investor, there is no reason to jump into that hornet's nest. Some people watch the late night news and then submit an order. At least if you are going to do that, use a limit order; otherwise, the big guys will take you to the cleaners. They will move the price to where they need it to go so that they can make money and then fill your order at that price. It's a killer thing for investors, and people do it all the time. It's better to wait an hour and take care of business on your terms. By sending your order in ahead of time, you are just helping them take your money, and worse, you are contributing to the advantage they have by giving them a bigger picture of the market.

The thing about the openings is that there is a distinct advantage at that particular moment of the trading day for larger investors, larger institutions, and so on. The problem is that they have a better view of what is going on than the smaller investors, just by nature of their size. It's as if everyone was going to the same grocery store, but some people were buying for themselves, and some people were buying for a huge restaurant chain, like McDonalds or something. Obviously, the person with the grocery list for McDonalds knows more about what items will be in short supply at the store than the rest of us. A buyer who needs ketchup, to give an example, knows the store will run out of ketchup before even walking in the door because he or she has a big order. Big institutions and market makers also have big orders, so they know before trading even commences that if they have to buy, say, IBM or something, then IBM also will be in high demand. Hence, at the opening what you have is a bunch of big players, big institutional and market making buyers and sellers, all whom know that they will be moving a stock price, and this can allow them to manipulate markets very easily. By the time the rest of the market figures out what is going on with the buy and sell orders of these big institutions, it may be too late, or just not worth entering the trade. With this type of informational advantage, it's best to stay away from the openings, unless one is really committed to getting in and out of trades quickly and tolerating risk. The openings are one situation where size does matter.

GLOSSARY

10k   The annual report a public company is required to file for its shareholders.

10q   The quarterly report a public company is required to file for its shareholders.

All or none   An order to purchase or sell a security in which the broker/dealer is instructed to fill the entire order or not to fill it at all.

Amex   American Stock Exchange.

Analyst   An individual employed by large brokerage firms who analyzes the fundamentals of a company and issues earnings expectations and other information relating to a company's stock.

Arbitrage   A transaction in which, given that the same security is selling at two different prices, "the security" is bought at the lower price and resold at the higher price.

Ask price   The price at which market participants offer to sell a security.

Auction market   A market such as the New York Stock Exchange, where trading occurs in one place and a specialist makes markets and provides liquidity.

Balance sheet   The financial statement that lists the assets, liabilities, and shareholder's equity of a company at a specific point in time.

Basis point   A measure of interest rates, where one basis point is $\frac{1}{100}$ of 1 percent.

Bear   A trader who expects market prices to decline. A trader can also be described as *bearish*.

Bear market   A market with declining prices.

Bid   The price a market maker or investor who subscribes to an ECN is willing to pay for a Nasdaq stock.

Bond   An investment instrument in which the seller of the bond agrees to pay back the price of the bond as well as a premium.

Bookmark   A way to save a URL for a specific Web site in a folder in order to have fast access to it in the future.

Bounce   A redirection in the market that occurs when there is a serious down movement followed by a serious upswing.

Broker   A financial intermediary who brings buyers and sellers together and charges commissions.

Browser   The software that allows an individual to access Web sites. Examples include Netscape Navigator, Microsoft Internet Explorer, and Opera.

Bull   A trader who expects market prices to increase.

Bull market   A market with increasing prices.

Chat   The ability to email back and forth in an instant message format.

Cheap talk   A term that refers to the ability to send out signals; e.g., a threat to veto a bill by the President is considered cheap talk.

Commission   The charge a broker collects for serving as the intermediary in a financial transaction.

Cookies   The ability of a Web site owner to track your preferences and movement within the site.

Correction A term referring to a fall in the market of less than 20 percent.

Coupon The interest that is paid to a bondholder for a bond.

Covering the position Closing a position by buying back the stock that a trader sold short.

Day order An order that is specified to be filled within the day it is placed or else canceled.

Day trader A trader who closes out all positions at the end of the day for cash.

Dealer-driven market A market, such as the Nasdaq, where multiple market makers compete against each other as providers of liquidity.

Downbid A decrease of one level in the price of a stock on the Nasdaq.

Downtick A decrease in the price of a stock on the NYSE of one level, in which a trade has taken place.

DPOs Direct public offerings.

DPPs Direct purchase plans.

DRIPs Dividend reinvestment plans.

DSL A way to access the Internet much faster than with a normal modem line.

ECN Electronic communication network. Investors presented on bid and offer of stock who purchase and sell the stocks in which they are trading. ECNs sometimes represent market makers, but they are not subjected to SOES. They only accept preference orders.

Equity Ownership in a firm, for example, by owning stock issued by a firm.

Flat Net value equals zero. This is used to refer to profits and positions currently held.

Fundamentals Information relating to a company, which is used to predict the success and profitability of a company by some market participants. Some fundamentals may be debt ratio, market share, etc.

Gap When a stock price opens at a different price than it closed the previous day.

Good-till-canceled An order with a restriction that stipulates that the order is in effect until it is canceled.

GTC   An order that is good till canceled.

GTX   An order that is good till executed.

High bid   When a market maker or ECN wants to pay higher for a stock than anyone else and increases the current bid price. The high bid is the act of increasing the bid price.

Hit the bids   A term used when a trader wants to sell a stock on the bid.

Income statement   A financial statement that reports operating results such as net income for a given period.

Index fund   A mutual fund whose basket of stocks is the same as the basket used by some market index of securities.

Inside market   The current price range of a stock. It is shown as the current bid by the current offer.

Institutional investor   A term used to refer to firms that invest in the stock market, instead of individuals.

IPO   Initial public offering. When a company offers its shares to the public.

IRA   Individual retirement account. A trust fund into which any employee can put $2000 per year.

ISDN   Integrated Services Digital Network. ISDN delivers information much faster than a normal phone line.

ISP   Internet service providers (ISPs) are companies that provide the link that lets an individual get online. There are both local and national ISPs, and the choice as to which to select is up to the individual.

Leverage   A term referring to debt, often used to describe how much of an investment or position is financed by borrowing.

Limit order   An order to be filled only at a price no worse than a specified price level, called the *limit price.*

Liquidity   The ability to enter/exit an investment or make a transaction quickly and at low costs because there are buyers and sellers willing to take opposite positions.

Listed stocks   Stocks sold on the NYSE.

Long position   When an investor owns a stock, in anticipation of a price increase. Selling stock that one owns is called a *long sale.*

Low offer When a market maker or ECN wants to sell a stock lower than anyone else and lowers the current offer price. The low offer is the act of decreasing the offer price.

Market capitalization The stock price multiplied by the number of shares outstanding. Also known as *market cap*.

Market maker A market participant responsible for providing liquidity, i.e., stands ready to buy or sell from traders.

Market order An order to be filled immediately as it is placed and at the current market prices.

Market risk The risk that the value of any one stock will be affected by the general value of other assets on the market.

Message boards Available at many sites, these are like bulletin boards where users post a comment or a question and other users post responses. Message boards exist online for virtually any topic you can think of.

Money market The market for securities with short-term maturity, usually less than 1 year.

Mutual fund A company that invests the aggregate money of its shareholders in the markets.

NASD National Association of Securities Dealers. The organization whose member firms make markets in the Nasdaq markets.

NYSE New York Stock Exchange.

Offer The price at which a market maker offers to sell a stock.

Open outcry The system of trading stocks in which individuals gather around a prespecified trading area and shout out the bids and offers.

Order flow A term referring to the stream of buying amounts observed by, for example, a specialist on the NYSE. Another example would be large brokerage firms who observe internal order flow from their clients.

Overlying offer A list of market makers and ECNs that are offering to sell the stock but are not on the current offer.

Over-the-counter A market for securities in which trading occurs off an organized exchange among brokers and investors.

Preference order An order to buy or sell that is only entered to and seen by a specific market maker or ECN and is not open for anyone else to see or to execute.

Primary market   The market for securities when they are offered initially to the public and have not been traded previously.

Profit taking   When a sell-off of some stock ensues because investors feel that the price is high and they want cash instead of the stock.

Pure discount bond   A bond such as a Treasury bill that pays no coupon but sells at a discount from its par value.

Quote   The description of the market for a stock, which includes bid and ask prices, as well as the size of the quantities supplied and demanded at those prices.

Rally   When the price of a stock steadily increases.

Resistance   A price level that represents a psychological barrier for the market, beyond which the price of a stock cannot rise. Often, when a stock reaches the resistance level, investors fear that the price will fall, as it has before, and sell, which causes the price to fall.

Return   The increase in wealth (often measured as a percent) due to investing in some asset.

Risk-free rate   The return of an asset with no risk.

Risk premium   The return above the risk-free rate that investors demand for assuming some asset risk.

S1   The statement a company files when it plans on going public.

Scalper   A trader who derives profits from holding assets just long enough to exploit arbitrage opportunities that arise from small price changes.

Search engine   An online robot that helps you find different Web sites on the Internet. Examples include Lycos and Infoseek.

SEC   Securities and Exchange Commission. The regulating body of the securities industry and exchanges.

Secondary market   The market for assets that were issued previously and trade among investors.

Sell-off   When a large number of shares are offered in the market for a stock, causing its price to fall.

Shorting   Selling a security that you do not own in the hopes that its value will decrease in price, at which point you can repurchase it.

Short sale   A sale of an asset that is borrowed from a broker and later repurchased from the market and returned to the broker. The idea of a short sale is to borrow stock to sell while the price is high and later buy back to replace the borrowed stock when the price is low.

SOES Small Order Execution System. A trading system that allows investors to purchase and sell stocks immediately after they enter an order. The number one benefit is immediate executions.

SOES'ed out The term for entering a SOES order and not receiving a print (execution).

Specialist The individual who is in charge of making markets and providing liquidity for stocks traded on the NYSE.

SPIC Securities Investment Protection Corporation. Insurance for online brokers.

Spread The difference between the bid price and the ask price.

Stock index A measure of the performance of a stock market or some sector of the stock market consisting of an averaging of some or all of the stocks traded in the market or sector.

Stop limit order Used when the top price is reached or passed on a limit order.

Stop order An order that calls for a transaction to be filled until the stock price reaches the stop price.

Support A price level that represents a psychological barrier for the market, beyond which the price of a stock cannot fall. Often, when a stock reaches the support level, investors assume that the price will increase, as it has before, and buy, which causes the price to increase.

Swing A sudden and dramatic redirection of the market.

T1/T3 A way to access the Internet that is much faster than with a normal modem line.

Take the offers When a trader wants to buy a stock on the offer.

Technical analysis Analyzing the behavior of stock price movements over time by way of stock price charts and graphs.

Underlying bid A list of market makers and ECNs who are willing to buy the stock but are not on the current bid.

Underwriter The group that buys the new issue of securities from the issuing corporation and resells it to the public.

Upbid An increase in the price of a stock on the Nasdaq of one level.

Uptick   An increase in the price of a stock on the NYSE of one level, in which a trade has taken place.

URL   Uniform Resource Locator. URLs are simply the addresses of Web sites. They start with *http://* and most of the time follow that with a *www.* (which stands for World Wide Web). They then have the domain name, which includes the specific name of the site, and then are followed by a *.com* or *.net* or another ending that tells you where the address is located, e.g., *.uk* for the United Kingdom.

Yield   The discount rate for a bond, which equates the present value of the coupons paid by the bond and the principal to the price.

Zero-plus tick   When a trade takes place on the NYSE for some stock in which price has not changed but in the previous change, price had increased.

BIBLIOGRAPHY

Chance, Don. *An Introduction to Derivatives*. Fort Worth: The Dryden Press, 1998.

Copeland, Thomas E., and J. Fred Weston. *Financial Theory and Corporate Policy*. New York: Addison-Wesley Publishing Company, 1992.

Huang, Chi-fu, and Robert Litzenberger. *Foundations for Financial Economics*. Englewood, New Jersey: Prentice-Hall, 1988.

Malkiel, Burton G. *A Random Walk Down Wall Street*. New York: W.W. Norton & Company, 1990.

Mishkin, Frederic S. *The Economics of Money, Banking, and Finanical Markets*. New York: Addison-Wesley Publishing Company, 1997.

Scott, David L. *Wall Street Words*. Boston: Houghton Mifflin Company, 1988.

INDEX

ABOUT THE AUTHOR

Rafael Romeu teaches economics and banking at the University of Maryland. In addition to his research on global equity and foreign exchange markets, Romeu is an experienced manager of private sector pension funds.

www.ingramcontent.com/pod-product-compliance
Lightning Source LLC
Chambersburg PA
CBHW011302210326
41599CB00035B/7094